Tro

The Tactical Secrets of Lake Fishing

Ed Rychkun

hancock

house

ISBN 0-88839-338-5
EAN 9780888393388
Copyright © 1994 Ed Rychkun

Second printing 2006

Cataloging in Publication Data
Rychkun, Ed
    Trout fishing

    ISBN 0-88839-338-5

    1. Trout fishing. 2. Trolling (Fishing) I. Title.
SH687.R92 1994   799.1'755   C94-910314-4

Printed in Indonesia—TK PRINTING

Published simultaneously in Canada and the United States by

HANCOCK HOUSE PUBLISHERS LTD.
19313 Zero Avenue, Surrey, B.C. Canada V3S 9R9
(604) 538-1114 Fax (604) 538-2262

HANCOCK HOUSE PUBLISHERS
1431 Harrison Avenue, Blaine, WA U.S.A 98230-5005
(604) 538-1114 Fax (604) 538-2262

Website: **www.hancockhouse.com**
Email: **sales@hancockhouse.com**

CONTENTS

FIGURES AND TABLES

DEDICATION

This book is dedicated to my brother and best friend, Mike.

To me there is no finer example of an angler who places the sport of fishing in its appropriate stature. Without Mike, I would have never been inspired to convey the enjoyment of fishing. His tenacious dedication to perfecting the analytical process of seeking out that elusive big fish has always left me in wonder. This persistence has only been rivaled by his professional abilities as an engineer. And yet, I have seen him, time and time again, bubble with excitement even when the small ones nibbled at his hook. But more important, Mike has taught me to enjoy the sport of fishing regardless of the outcome—perhaps the philosophical side to fishing. His wry humor, his constant grin, and his dedication to enjoyment indeed add to the fun, but his persistence is what really inspired me to see magic in its final simplicity—that which we all consider as secrets. Sharing this with Mike is a unique and wonderful experience.

I am forever grateful for this opportunity and am particularly proud to be able to convey these little secrets to others so that they may also enjoy the sport to the same degree.

INTRODUCTION

Have you ever wondered what makes the difference between an expert fisherman and an average one? You may have spotted "experts" occasionally without knowing it. They are the quiet, cool-looking, aloof gents who never seem to be carrying much gear with them. They seem to fish in a different dimension than us average fellows, picking fish out of the most unsuspecting spots. They seem to be at peace with nature, totally oblivious to anything else.

But there is another, different characteristic that these experts have. They need a very limited supply of items to catch fish—big ones! And whatever it is that they need seems to be contained in their pockets, not in enormous tackle boxes. They seem to apply technology, not use it. One thing is clear, they know what they are doing and they do not need many devices to be productive. They have some very clear answers on where they should fish, when they should fish, and what they should use to fish. They seem to have simplified the whole process of fishing.

But the irony of all this is that once they become experts, they can publish a book. And that book always seems to drop us back one level before things got simple. The expert is free to create vast volumes on how to fish. That is where we average fellows become exposed to the experts. Perhaps that is the expert's prerogative...make things complicated again. So what an expert says is very often not what he does; unfortunately you can't be an expert if you have only simple things to say, can you?

Mike and I have always classified ourselves as average fisherman. We are not yet "experts," but we have logged a considerable amount of water time, and we have learned to reduce a lot of voluminous information down to some simple tactics and "secrets." So we don't take a vast inventory of angling apparatus with us any more, and we don't believe in making things complicated any more, either. Fortunately we found a publisher who also feels the same way. So we decided to share our tactics and secrets, keeping them specific to the most popular angling pastime...trolling for trout.

Why choose trolling? Trolling has become a very popular fishing option. Any angler with a boat and a bit of trolling expertise is a major threat to any trout. A troller who understands a few key secrets, and is willing to experiment in a trial-and-error process, can get to his target extremely fast. If you add some basic knowledge about the habits and habitats of fish, that troller can out fish any other angler who is using other fishing techniques on the same body of water. The fact is that some key fundamentals combined with the trolling technique can make up a most deadly method. Concentrations of fish can be pinpointed quite rapidly. A troller is quite capable of trolling a whole body of water in a dragnet pattern at different depths and inevitably catch fish; but there is always the desire, and the challenge, to locate more fish quicker, and to tangle with the larger ones. Locating those fish quickly is precisely what this book is all about—so you don't have to dragnet the whole body of water.

Much has been written about the many ways of fishing the different species of game fish. The tendency has been to create encyclopedias of information on fishing, with the usual result of providing too much information to use when it comes to locating *that* fish on *that* body of water you have selected. More often than not, your interest is more specific to certain areas, fish, or even technique. Not only that, but *how to fish* is not usually the issue; *how to catch fish* is the more important issue. We thought that some totally different information was needed to deal with more specific issues. Because we have always tried to keep fishing simple and enjoyable, we have focused on tactics and a handful of what we call secrets. Actually, these are not really secrets; they are simple and logical processes, once someone has told you what they are: processes which nevertheless seem to come to you only after many years of fishing. This book will share with you these simple angling secrets that will help you increase your chances of finding and catching fish. To do this, we focus on trolling and the more popular game fish, trout. This book is not designed to teach you to fish. It is designed to teach you how to catch fish. How do we do this? We just tell you how to answer the same simple questions that every angler wants answered, mainly:

Where should I fish?
What do I fish with?
When do I fish?

These three simple questions are always in the back of your mind, particularly after you spend hours, and even days, being "skunked." Despite the fact that you go fishing to enjoy the beauty, serenity, and peaceful interlude with nature, somehow seeing the other guys drag in the big ones has a bit of a dampening effect on that enjoyment.

There is another plight to our story. We disagree with the current trend in the "sport" of fishing. Our world of angling has turned into a technical jungle of sophisticated depth sounders, fish finders, electronic gizmos, and a multitude of expensive high-tech apparatus that always promises to get you to the big ones. I recently picked up a fishing catalogue and was absolutely amazed at the electronic devices available to scan for the fish schools, plot three-dimensional underwater topography, and even create electronic vibrations. Is this really a sport? What about the simple rod and reel? Is the fish the intelligent one? Why do we need all this high-tech apparatus anyway? It gets a bit discouraging to pick up books which give you all the "secrets" that involve using an expensive down rigger, fish finder, and other expensive devices— just to catch a few rainbow trout. Seriously! What has happened to the simple life that fishing used to reflect?

So, if you are looking for secrets that tell you how to use those devices, this book is not for you. Buy a book by the experts. We are concerned about how to catch fish through tactics. We are not concerned with how to use the equipment. We are concerned with the simple application of the basic equipment, and some key tactics that we have discovered the old way—by trial and error. Mike and I have fished a lot of years and a lot of places. It took a long time to develop a "keep it simple" routine for maximizing your chances of catching fish and minimizing your searching time. We call these *tactical secrets*.

Mike and I decided to structure this book to reflect the way we searched for answers in the beginning. After spending many years of catching few fish, we began to think that we were fishing in the wrong places, we were using the wrong things, or we were not fishing at the right time. The time, place, and technique questions are simple reflections of the fundamental questions of when, where, and what. When should we fish, where should we fish, and what should we use to fish?

Well we, as average fishermen, have spent many years wondering why we have spent so many fruitless hours on the water when we are supposed to be smarter than a fish—after all, I was an educated mathematician, Mike was an educated analytical engineer, so how could these fish continuously get away from us? When we really thought about it, we realized we were using our instinct to answer the crucial questions. We fished when we thought it was a good time. This was typically when we felt like it or when the weather was right for us. We fished where we thought the fish might be, and we fished with what we thought the fish would like to eat. This process was just an instinctual assessment based on our feelings, not the fish's. We figured that we were the smart ones so we could fool the fish with our smart selections...how could any fish resist the temptation of the colorful Army Navy special? Well, you know the answer. So we started to develop some simple criteria about when, where, and what.

We have chosen a simple format to do this. The book is divided into major chapters that focus on the where, the what, and the when questions—simply because those are the questions that need to be answered. Each chapter is then designed to cover a simple *secret*, the *tactics* behind it, a discussion of the *concepts* and *application*, and an example—*out on the water*. Please bear in mind that our examples are just that—examples, and they do not always illustrate the precise set of conditions that always work. Remember that we are teaching tactics, not rules. The real science of fishing is in the process and tactics employed. This process is one of deductive reasoning and just figuring out a way to get to the right spot, the right depth, and the right bait, regardless of place or conditions.

Before getting into some of the specifics of the where, when, and what aspects of angling, we are going to consider some very fundamental things that will help you make the hunting process efficient. Much of this is wrapped up in your ability to reason, what you know about your quarry, and how you use your equipment. Sound simple? It is. Like many other situations, man has a tendency to over complicate things rather than simplify them. The fact is that very few people really take advantage of some simple fundamentals. Let's have a look at some of these.

1   SOME FUNDAMENTALS

This Chapter deals with some simple fundamentals of fishing. You have no doubt heard it before, but this time we are going to tell it a bit differently. When it comes to fishing, there are three key elements that you need to consider, namely you, the fish, and your equipment. These, more often than not, are not considered with any degree of seriousness since the average fisherman just assumes that he is smart, the fish is primitive, and the equipment is just equipment.

First of all, let us look closely at you, the fisherman. Being a member of the human race, you are supposed to possess the ability of superior intelligence and rational thought. This is no doubt why you are always outwitting those simple-minded fish. The truth is that you need to understand that catching fish is an elimination process that involves finding a smaller and smaller volume of water within which that fish swims, then finding the right time to offer him the right meal. This process of finding the quarry is precisely what the human can do well, so it is a good idea to use this capability.

The second element is the fish, your quarry. The fish may be less intelligent but he has some superior equipment to offset his inability to think. Such equipment, in the form of superior senses, provides him with survival ability that functions almost automatically and instinctively, making him faster than you are. So the fish will typically outwit you because you cannot find him, or you offer him stupid things, or he has effective sensory equipment to detect a scam. To deal with this, you need to better understand the fish, his capabilities, his habits, and his habitat.

The third element is your equipment, your chosen aids. These will assist you in the actual process of fishing. Once you understand that you need to apply a process of elimination, and once you know the habits of your quarry, there are some key things that your simple equipment, and its application, can do to help you to seek out those elusive fish.

Enough said. Let us get to the purpose. As you proceed through this chapter, keep these three things in mind. It will help you keep a fresh, simple perspective.

1.1   APPLY A PROCESS OF ELIMINATION

Tactics. The process of elimination is a premeditated method of arriving at a desired objective by successive elimination of wrong answers. This process is a crucial way of seeking out the where, when, and what answers of fishing.

Concepts and Application. One of the most fundamental realizations of fishing is that you are never able to have all the answers. You need to make some mistakes, in a trial-and-error process, to get to the right conclusion. The best way to do this is to use a process of eliminating the wrong areas, depths, and baits as quickly as possible. The process of elimination is a term used to describe a method of reaching an objective in a step-wise progression. For example, you would follow a process of elimination in finding the fish. We actually use a process of elimination quite automatically in our day-to-day lives, but we seldom apply a *process* of elimination.

With regard to fishing, let's take a simple case: you have heard about the rainbow trout that have a voracious tendency to bite lures in half in this serene little lake up in the mountains. All you have to do, you have heard, is drive up there and drag the right lure in front of the biggest fish in the lake. Ironically, you would use the process of elimination in the steps you take to get to the lake—but that is where the process typically ends.

There are, in fact, just ten simple steps and decisions that progressively put you into a more and more specific space, time, and tactic. Consider the selection process when you go fishing:

Step	Selection	Decision
1.	Select the fish of interest	say the fish is trout
2.	Select a fishing area	say British Columbia
3.	Select an area in B.C.	say around Kamloops
4.	Select a lake to fish in	say Rainbow Lake
5.	Select the best time to fish	say Saturday morning
6.	Select the area of the lake	say the west end
7.	Select a method of fishing	say trolling
8.	Select the type of bait to use	say flatfish
9.	Select the fishing depth	say 20 feet down
10.	Select the trolling pattern	say in a circle

You are using an elimination process to select the appropriate lake by rejecting other alternatives. You have eliminated all other lakes in the vast area of B.C. in favor of a specific body of water. But to get to the fish in that body of water, you need to apply a process of selection that leads you to a very specific section of water. In most instances, the process will involve three aspects that become more and more detailed. The first aspect deals with space, as you select a smaller and smaller area to fish in. The next aspect deals with time, as you select a more and more specific segment of time to fish within. And the third is the aspect of tactics, as you determine what you should use and how you will use it.

When you get to the lake, however, the process typically becomes one of random trial and error. At the lake, you have a new objective: of finding *that* little volume of water, and the right bait so that you can drag it in front of the fish.

The key to this is to realize that you need to apply a process of elimination to find the right place, time, and bait before you will get a strike from a fish. This will involve making mistakes to find those right answers. What you want to do is make as few mistakes as possible to get to them.

On the Water. It was the first morning of our fishing trip. The sky was clear, the birds were chirping, and the lake was as smooth as a mirror. The smell of bacon in the camp air gave the morning the final crown. Mike's wife Bev was selecting the book to read in the boat, while my wife Hope was enjoying her third cup of coffee. Mike was rummaging through his new flatfish box. It was time to test our skills. It was now 7:00 A.M. and you could hear the purr of outboards on the lake. Mike couldn't stand it any longer. "Ed, we've got to get out there, I can feel the big one biting. I know exactly where they are this time—I have a hot feeling for this silver and black flatfish." Grabbing the rod and the tackle box, I downed my coffee and said, "All right let's go."

At 7:15 we were on the lake. Now where would we fish with Mike's special flatfish? "OK Ed, this flatfish is hot, but since I am not sure about the color, why don't you try an orange one? Since it's early morning, I think the fish may be down about 20 feet, so I am going to troll with 2 weights and 50 pulls. Why don't you go for 50 pulls and 1 weight, Ed? The sun is still behind that mountain and the water looks fairly deep along that side, so let's troll along that shoreline."

After 10 minutes of trolling and no action, I said, "Mike, I'm going down deeper with 3 weights."

"OK," Mike said, "I'll go 10 more pulls but I am going to change to a blue and red, then head toward that bay over there."

After 15 more minutes, and no action, I said: "Well I think we should take a sweep around the bay one more time. There is no action at these depths on this flatfish, so I am going back up to the top with a Spratley."

After 50 pulls and 5 minutes, I felt a nibble on the line. "Mike, I just had a nibbler back there. I think we should take another sweep over that area and you should come back up close to surface with your flatfish."

"Ok, I'll go for 1 weight and 60 pulls."

About 3 minutes into the sweep over the same area, Mike's rod showed a quick jerk, followed by a silver flash about 75 feet back as the trout rose to surface trying to spit the plug. "Faaantaaastic!" Mike shouted. "What a beauty! Get the net ready—"

After some intense action, the 15-inch trout was in the net. I had reeled in.

"Congratulations Mike, you got the hot item, blue and red, 60 pulls and 1 weight, right? Let's go over the same area. You got any more blue and reds?"

The process of elimination started with selecting the plug and the strip of water. The next step was to try different depths, and different bait. Once a nibble was felt, you obviously had a success that would eliminate the other trials, and the area of interest was more specific. Once a strike was made, the rest was obvious. There were some mistakes made but the process of elimination worked to get to the target. We had figured out where, when, and what in 33 minutes.

1.2 UNDERSTAND YOUR QUARRY

Tactics. The gamefish has some highly developed sensory organs that it uses for survival. Knowing the limitations and capabilities of these not only reveals the basic habits of the fish but it also provides ways in which fishing may be best applied.

Concepts and Application. The second most important fundamental realization is that the fish is rarely understood enough to be caught easily. One of the greatest failures of anglers is to not understand the basic habits, instincts, and behavior of their quarry. Technically, this is a science called physiology, the study of the functions of living organisms—how they eat, breath, and move, and what they do to keep alive. Very few fishermen ever take the time to understand what makes a fish tick. Let's face it, if you knew that fish never ate sandwiches then you wouldn't waste time making any for them to try. Sounds a bit ridiculous but think of the time you could waste offering a fish the wrong fly, simply because it doesn't recognize it as a known food item? And you wouldn't fish in a certain section of the lake if you knew that fish did not like to stay there because it lacked oxygen. The fact remains that there are numerous things about the fish's habits and abilities that govern where he is most likely to hang out. Knowing this can help you to understand what you should or should not do to catch them. By having a better understanding of the fish's behavior, anatomical aspects, and instincts, you can increase your chances of answering the where, when, and what questions. Fish behave a certain way because of their makeup. Knowing this will help you save time and effort. It will allow you to apply the process of elimination much more effectively.

As a starter, let us simply point out the key items about gamefish that most people do not know, but have always wondered about. Just consider some of these little tidbits of information. Did you know that:

Fish have a highly developed sense of smell
Fish are cold-blooded animals
Fish have preferred temperature ranges
Fish are sensitive to small temperature changes
Fish have a tasting ability on their snouts

Fish are near sighted but can adjust their eyes to longer vision
Fish can see well at night, particularly in the moonlight
Fish can spit out bait if it does not have a recognizable taste
Fish lose muscle energy rapidly and must rest to restore it
Fish prefer slow water to conserve energy
Fish feed in a daily rhythm
Fish can memorize smells, sounds, vibrations, and images
Fish have two sophisticated ways of sound detection
Fish can sense and locate sound vibrations
Fish have a highly developed sense of taste
Fish need several hours to half a day to digest food
Fish must conserve energy so they seldom waste it
Fish stay as close to food sources as possible
Fish stay as near to shelter or cover as possible
Fish can distinguish colors
Fish can see at night because they can change to night vision
Fish take about two hours to change from day to night vision
Fish have inactive and active periods
Fish can go into semi-hibernation because of cool temperature

Do some of these explain why you have not caught as many fish as you would like to? Perhaps you underestimated the fish's abilities? These are all key things to know about fish, in that they tell you how the animal survives within, and reacts to, its environment. Knowing more about these habits will help you determine how to catch him more easily.

The point to this section is to convey that knowing more about the fish gives you a decided advantage in that you are able to predict where he might hang out, what he prefers to eat, and how you should present it to him. This will become apparent in the following chapters, where each of the above characteristics will be explained in much more detail, within the context of where, when, and what. Many of the simple secrets are based on the fish's physiological makeup and his simple need to survive.

On the Water. It was high noon and we left the dock with an eagerness that had to get us our limits. This was our first day on the lake, and we hadn't killed ourselves to get out too early. You could see the odd boat with netting action. Mike and I decided to cruise down to the north end of the lake to try our luck. This was where the big ones were—so we were told.

"Well, where to Mike?," I asked. "You've had your nose buried in that fish ecology book for two days now, so what are the chances of using science instead of luck for a change?"

Mike looked at me with a wry squint. "I see it like this—the sun is high toward the south, just over that mountain. They don't like bright sun so a good area is where the shade is along that mountain. Since the air is warm, they will probably be in the lower part of the thermocline, at about 40 feet down. Since rainbow trout prefer temperatures around 60 degrees, they will be at this level. There is a creek emptying into the area, over by the rock bluffs, a sure sign of a food area, particularly since there is quite a bit of vegetation there, so the oxygen will attract them. If my guess is right, I would say that the cooler thermocline intersects the underwater rock bluffs in that bay. I would say that we should troll in a deep sweep through the bay about 50 feet away from the shoreline. I'll use a willow leaf and a worm. If there are any fish in this area of the lake, then they will smell these delicious worms, because of their sense of smell. The willow leaf will also help attract them because the lateral line will pick up the vibrations and they will also be able to see the flash of the leaves, thinking they are fish. This way I am going to take advantage of four sensory organs and two instincts. I don't like using this hardware and smelly worms but, I promise, once we find the hot spot, I will convert to flies—honest, Ed."

The point of this example is that there are some specific things about fish habits that reveal the type of habitat that they would find most suitable. And within this area of water, using things that give *them* the best possibility of locating the bait will offer *you* your best chances. Knowing these physiological needs helps you to decide where the best location will be and also suggests, in itself, the best fishing strategy. Otherwise, you would just drag your best "guess" around the lake.

16

1.3   MONITOR THE DISTANCE

Tactics. Your fishing reel is a simple device that can allow you to measure and control the length of line that is being released. This leads to effective depth and distance control, which are crucial to finding the fish habitats

Concepts and Application. It is important to note that your basic reel has much more to it than first meets the eye. It is actually a fantastic piece of equipment with some useful properties, offering you several ways to control line distance. Controlling and monitoring line distance is the next important fundamental requirement of fishing. This will become more and more evident in the following chapters when the process is actually applied. For the current discussion, let us consider a few of the simple techniques that allow you to measure and monitor the amount of line that you let out.

Your reel allows you to set tension and to release line. It is important to know how much line is out at all times since it is the key means of remembering the proper depth. There are a few simple secrets that let you control this effectively. The first technique is the "pull technique." If you ever see an expert, you will observe him pulling line out from the reel in short pulls. The typical "pull" will result in about 18 inches of line being pulled out of the reel. The procedure is to set the tension low, hold the rod in one hand, set the weight in the water, and begin pulling the line out with the other hand, each time grabbing the line just at the reel and pulling to let the line out into the water. The average pull, unless you are a long-armed ape, is about 18 inches, so each pull will release about 18 inches (or 1.5 feet) of line into the water. This becomes a reasonably easy arithmetic problem for most of us average fellows so that ten pulls will release 15 feet. In this way you can let out a predictable amount of line.

Another effective method is to measure exactly how much line is released by one rotation of the reel handle. The average-sized spinning reel will also release about 18 inches. Although this will vary a bit as the line is let out, the variation is not that significant. The beauty of the spinning reel handle method is that it gives you dual control. You can release a known distance and you can pull in a known distance. This means that if you want to change to a shorter known length of line, you don't have to reel in all the line and then "pull" out again.

On the water. We were at the south end of the lake. This was a new spot for us. You could see by the shoreline that the lake was probably deep along that edge. The other side looked shallow.

"Mike, let's take a few minutes and check out the depths of this area. A survey line across the lake and one down the middle should give us a good feel."

Taking the boat to the deepest shore, I then took out a 2-ounce bell sinker and tied it on to the line. Hanging the sinker over the side, I let the reel go into reverse and let the weight drop. At 40 rotations, I could feel the light thump on the bottom. "That makes it 60 feet if I use one and a half feet per rotation. Let me reel in and let's move out about 100 feet." The next thump was at 50 turns, or 75 feet, and the next was at 60. Following in a line, the next was 15, and we could see weeds along the shoreline, so a sloping bottom was likely. Doing the same up the middle, we could see that a channel of about 110 feet was true for about 1,000 feet.

"OK, let's troll right up the middle. I am going to let out 100 pulls, with a one-ounce weight. That's about 150 feet and it should give me a depth of about 30 feet. Why don't you do the same with two ounces to get deeper, probably at about 40 to 45 feet? If that doesn't work, then we can crank in 10 pulls and take another pass through the area."

The reel handle turns are being used to survey the lake bottom. Pulls could have been just as effective but a little slower. The reel is being used to a distinct advantage. Now let us take a look at another important part of your fishing equipment.

1.4 READ YOUR ROD TIP

Tactics. Your rod tip is a sensitive device that can reflect the specific vibrations set up by the bait or gear being trolled behind the boat. By careful attention to the right pattern evident in the rod tip, you can easily determine when a wrong pattern is in progress, saving much time and allowing corrective action.

Concepts and Application. Another simple but useful overlooked fundamental resides in the use of your rod tip. Your lure, bait, or whatever you are dragging, has a characteristic feel, or vibration, to it as it rotates, spins, or wiggles against the current. Just as the fish is able to detect and recognize the vibration patterns, so should you—by reading the tip. Each lure is designed to simulate a realistic movement in the water, or create vibrations which are picked up by the fish's sensory system. You can spare yourself a lot of wasted time if you pay attention to the rod tip and note what this "typical" vibration looks like. If, for example, you place the lure, say a flatfish, into the water as the boat moves, you will see that it exhibits a certain wiggle. If you speed up the boat, you will make it wiggle faster, or you may make it miss a wiggle and do a flip, even make it lose its regular rhythm, flip and tangle. If your speed is too slow, it may not wiggle well at all. The key is to note a speed where you can see a realistic wiggle, and note the regular movement of the rod tip. You may even feel it as you hold the rod. If you have something like a weed caught in the lure, or the lure has been twisted, the regularity will disappear, as will the regular movement of the tip. This is your signal that your bait is not able to do its job and that you need to check it.

On the Water. I had been trolling a flatfish for twenty minutes. Mike was hauling in his fourth fish and it was beginning to get a bit humiliating, to say the least. The girls were beginning to roll their eyes at each other more often, trying to contain a well of giggles that were building up. "What the hell is going on Mike?" I asked. "I am using the same plug as you are." Taking a side glance at the rod tip, my elderly brother looked smugly at me, like the joke about the old bull and the young bull on the hill, and said, "You know, I don't recognize that vibration at your rod tip. Are you sure that you aren't dragging a beer can instead of a flatfish? Ha Ha Ha." Taking a look at the tip, I could see that it did not have a constant vibration to it. Pulling it slightly showed a smooth pull to it, but no vibration like a flatfish should have given it as it wiggles. After pulling it in, the problem was obvious: the treble hook had caught itself on the line, completely destroying any possibility of a proper vibration. "You see, Ed, I told you—pay more attention to your rod tip and you won't waste so much time. Well girls, I've got my limit now, I guess we should go in for a beer; the fish have stopped biting anyway—"

The obvious thing was that the fish did not recognize the movement of the flatfish and the vibration (or lack of it) did nothing to get the fish's interest. Worst of all, I did not recognize it, because I simply did not read the rod tip. By the time I'd fixed it, the feeding period was finished.

1.5   KEEP YOUR HOOKS SHARP

Tactics. Your hooks and their ability to penetrate effectively requires that they have a very sharp point and a cutting edge. Since
these are dulled quickly, they must be sharpened constantly or
fish will be lost easily.

Concepts and Application. It is really difficult to count the number
of big fish that got away because we were too stupid about hooks
or too lazy to sharpen them. Fish have an uncanny ability to spit
the hook out when they realize they have been duped. A hook,
to be effective, must penetrate immediately when the fish takes
it or the possibility of losing the fish is very high. This is yet
another simple fundamental that is constantly overlooked. Let's
face it, after spending all that time getting a bite, it's foolish not
to maximize your chances of hauling the fish in. Just as a rough
rule of thumb, you will at least double your catch by keeping your
hooks sharp. Do you know any other ways of increasing your odds
so significantly?

The fact is that most anglers simply do not bother to consider
the hook, the most crucial item that keeps the fish on the line.
Hooks are designed to be razor sharp, but the points and edge
can be dulled incredibly easily. A majority of fish are lost because
of dull hooks. Hooks can be dulled by fish biting on them. They
can be dulled by friction against other things in your fish box,
against the floor, or any number of things that you would simply
not even bother to consider. Keeping your hooks sharp will increase your chances of keeping a fish on the line when it bites.

As a simple rule, sharpen your hook after two bites, or certainly after you have brought a fish in. Try a simple test by holding
your fingernail at a slight slope, about 30 degrees, and seeing if
your hook point is sharp enough to stay on the nail. If your hook
slips off, then it is too dull to use. Either sharpen it with the
sharpener in your tackle box, or throw it away and try a new one.
Do not waste time with dull hooks. It does not make much sense
to spend hundreds of dollars on a fishing trip and be cheap about
inexpensive hooks. Hooks must penetrate immediately upon the
slightest tug or they will surely spoil your trip.

Keeping sharp hooks, or keeping hooks sharp, whatever your

choice may be, is an important factor. You can increase your catch quite significantly by faithfully keeping them sharp.

The best way to sharpen a hook is to simply sweep it on a sharpening stone a few times on each side, then a few times on the back. Never do this back and forth—sharpen in one direction only, mainly toward the end point of the hook. It only takes a few seconds to do this. I repeat: the hook must be able to penetrate rapidly. The best way to ensure that this happens is to first give it a good point, and then give it razor edges so that it can cut in. Sharpen it in a triangular fashion so that you create a razor edge at the outside. This will create a cutting edge that will aid in cutting in when a bone is hit. Some hook sharpeners that you can buy have a V groove in them. These are the easiest to use in that they spare you the agony of poking yourself all the time.

On the Water. Mike and I have been trolling the lake for the last hour. Every time Mike gets a strike, he jumps up like a shot and reels in. The fish surfaces and then it is suddenly gone. "Dammit, what's going on? You've landed three fish in the last hour, Ed, and I've lost five!" Since Mike's line is still out, he pulls out about twenty more feet of line and sits down mumbling to himself. A few minute later, another strike. "God, what a strike! This one's a whale; he almost pulled the rod out of my hand! What? He's gone!" Once more, Mike sits down in disgust; he cracks an ale. He lets out five pulls and sits again. Five minutes later, his reel starts singing. "Look at this, Ed. He's huge—and heading for Vancouver!" Suddenly the line goes slack and Mike starts to reel in frantically. His reel handle is just a blur. "Good thing you've been weight lifting those beer, Mike; I've never seen such wrist action in my life." But the fish was running toward the boat. He surfaced, took a look at Mike, spit out the plug, and was gone.

Mike's dilemma was quite simple. Now I had a chance to get him back for his smug attitude about not watching my rod tip. "When did you sharpen your hook last, Mike?" I asked. "Oh jeez," he exploded in self-chastisement, "the action was so fast I didn't have time to sharpen the dammed thing."

1.6   ADJUST LINE TENSION

Tactics. Fish have the ability to taste and quickly reject any foreign objects that they have been fooled with and are very capable of spitting out hooks if the line is not set properly. You should always ensure that your line tension is not too tight or too loose to prevent fish loss.

Concepts and Application. Here is another fundamental problem that needs attention. Your reel has a tension control that is most often misused. The natural tendency is to set the tension tight, for fear of losing a fish. In fact, that is one of the best ways to lose a fish. There are numerous times when you will lose a fish because he just zoomed off, or because the line broke. The tension was too loose, or too tight. When it was too loose, the fish was free to dart away faster than you could reel in—and when you did, the fish was actually going out without any tension and was therefore free to spit the hooks out, at his leisure. When it was too tight, the fish panicked when he was still strong, either ripping the hook out of his mouth or breaking the leader. The moral of the story is that you need to always check your tension to see that you can pull the line out freely. Remember to set the tension: not too tight and not too loose.

On the Water. The lake was absolutely still. It was 8:00 P.M. and the fish were rising everywhere. Suddenly I could feel the rhythm of the plug cease, followed by a faint nibble. Almost instinctively I pulled up sharply and started to reel in. There was nothing. Ten pulls out and I sat down in an attempt to regain my composure. "Dammit! That's the third one that's done that to me. I'd better reel in and sharpen the hooks on that plug. This time I am not pulling; I will set the tension looser and let him go." Mike sat cool, just watching. After reeling in and carefully sharpening the hooks, I set the tension loose so I could pull it with two fingers easily. After forty pulls and five minutes, I could feel it again. This time I was cool. Wheeeeezzz went the line as it screamed out of the reel. I had a live one here. Then he broke surface, like a silver explosion, and was gone. I could see that he had run toward the boat so I started to reel in frantically. Too late, it was all over. Another beauty was gone.

At this point, Mike squinted a wary eye at me and began to giggle. "I can't stand this any longer. First you yank the hook out of his mouth before he has a chance to put it in his mouth, then when you finally let him sample it, you give him too much slack and he spits it out. Ed, that's pretty dumb since you have been giving me all this technical stuff about the dual sensing and tasting ability of these trout."

In this example the fish was having no freedom or too much freedom, two problems that can be handled by proper tension. Too tight or an early jerk and you've given him an early warning. Too loose and he has another chance to throw it.

You may consider these simple fundamentals as an insult to an angler's intelligence, but you should note that these six little concepts are the most commonly overlooked tactics in fishing! They may seem simple but if you employ them faithfully, the simple reality is that not only will you increase your chances of catching fish, but you also will decrease the amount of time wasted. These simple tactics are fundamental to answering the next important question: "Where do I fish?" Let's take a close look at this new question.

2   WHERE DO I FISH?

To answer the question on where to fish, you must solve two problems. You first need to select the right area to fish in and then you need to determine the best depth to fish at. The selection of area can most often be done through a visual analysis, but the selection of depth requires applying a process of elimination. In other words, there are certain identifiable spots on the lake where fish are most likely to hang out, and some of these can be determined by inspecting the water or land characteristics. The depth, however, is another matter since you cannot see what is below. Here you need to consider some different tactics to help select that water layer below surface which is most likely to harbor fish. The fact of the matter is that the fish will choose areas and depths that he prefers for certain reasons, so the best way to understand where this could be is best done by considering the fish's viewpoint. And the best way to consider a fish's viewpoint is to take a closer look at the fish's natural functions.

There are several factors that will determine the most likely fish hangout. First you must understand that trout do indeed "hang out." Fish will choose specific waters that will provide them with crucial environmental requirements, as dictated by their habits, needs, and basic survival instincts. Although we will elaborate on all of the fish's key sensory equipment when we discuss the *what* question in the next chapter, let us point out that trout have highly evolved instincts that are designed to deal with the five key survival requirements, namely:

Temperature	They need to keep their metabolism functioning
Oxygen	They need to find oxygen to breath
Food	They need to find food to live
Shelter	They need to avoid predators and harsh elements
Reproduction	They need to reproduce their species

With little by way of exception, fish will tend to seek out the water with the right aquatic environment that will best accommodate their primary physiological needs. To deal with this, they have evolved the appropriate abilities and basic instincts of survival that allow them to adjust to changes, but within limits, so will tend to stay in, or seek out, any environment that is suitable for them. Similarly, they will avoid an environment that is detected as hostile. Fish will have a natural tendency to find secure, comfortable areas in any body of water and these areas are the ones that you will most likely find them in. In this chapter, we will explore two important elements that control the fish's preferred location. These include the fish's basic survival needs and the fish's environment.

Temperature and oxygen levels represent the most immediate, serious problem to a fish. He needs to find water that has a specific temperature range. He also needs specific levels of oxygen to be present in the water in order to breathe. Since these can change with weather, this can represent a serious difficulty to both the fish and the angler. Similarly, food and shelter represent two other problems for the fish. These need to be found in sufficient abundance to allow survival. To explain how and why fish seek out specific areas of water, we will now look more closely at some of the fish's physiological functions and their relationship to the aquatic environment.

2.1 WATER TEMPERATURE IS CRUCIAL

Tactics. Each type of trout will have a preferred ideal temperature range within which its metabolism will function effectively. Fish will most likely feed and be found in these waters.

Concepts and Application. The first two primary requirements for the fish are to find the right temperature and to find sufficient oxygen. These are the most serious problems for a fish, tending to contribute heavily to a trout's decision on a preferred location. He must have the right combination of temperature and oxygen to survive. In looking more closely at why these are so critical, it must first be understood that a fish is a cold-blooded animal. This means that he does not have an "internal furnace" that uses food to keep the body temperature at a level needed for proper functioning. Rather, the fish has to rely on the external temperature to keep his body temperature at an acceptable level. If the fish's temperature gets too low, his metabolism will slow down to force inactivity, even semihibernation, as it does in winter. If it gets too high, the fish will suffer burnout or die. The rate of metabolism will control the fish's level of activity—and his rate of feeding. A fish's temperature will adjust to whatever the surrounding water temperature is, so the only way he can control his metabolism is to find the appropriate water temperature. If he cannot, then he will become inactive or fall victim to the elements. To help find appropriate temperature ranges, the fish is endowed with special sensing apparatus that helps him sense minute temperature variations in the water.

As an added inconvenience, fish need oxygen—so they must find areas where there is sufficient concentrated oxygen. Although they are capable of filtering out very minute particles of oxygen from the water, there is not typically an abundance of particles around. Oxygen levels will vary quite significantly, depending on many factors. For example, oxygen either mixes with the surface water from the air, or it is generated via photosynthesis as the underwater vegetation takes in sunlight and produces oxygen. But at night, water vegetation absorbs oxygen to produce carbon dioxide. Wind and temperature will also affect the rate at which the water and organic materials can absorb oxygen. All this makes it a fairly complicated life for the fish, since he is constantly looking for an environment that changes around him. The greatest influencing factor, however, is the temperature of the water, as affected by the temperature of the air. This has the most dramatic effect on the rate at which the oxygen in the air mixes with the water.

Oxygen, as pointed out, is crucial to a fish's survival. The fish does not need much, however, to survive, and it has some very sophisticated anatomy to extract the minute particles from the water. The particles get into the water in one of the two ways mentioned, either by mixing at the surface as water dissolves oxygen, or through photosynthesis where the vegetation takes sunlight and expels oxygen during the day. Typically, one liter of water has about one-thirtieth of its composition as oxygen. The solubility of oxygen decreases as water temperature increases, for example, there is a 50 percent decrease in the ability to take oxygen in going from a temperature of just around freezing to 80 degrees Fahrenheit. If the water is warm, the ability to take oxygen is significantly reduced, making it very hard for cold-water fish to breathe. If both air temperature and water temperature are cool, the ability to diffuse oxygen is good. If there is a lot of decaying matter, this will absorb oxygen. At night, plants take oxygen and expel carbon dioxide, so the good and bad areas can shift from time to time. There are also a few other factors that will contribute to shifting areas:

Turbulent waters pick up more oxygen by mixing
Wind mixes water with air
Cooler water absorbs more oxygen than warmer water
Surface water is usually well oxygenated but it sinks
Lower deep water depends on sinking oxygen
Underwater plants need oxygen
Oxygen becomes scarcer with depth

Because the fish are sensitive to temperature and require oxygen, they will tend to stay in a layer of water that they find suitable for them. This will change substantially according to the season, but the fish will always seek a place that provides him with an acceptable balance between temperature and oxygen. Thus, oxygen and temperature are considered the "lethal factors," meaning that if they get out of balance the result can be lethal to the fish. So the fish will instinctively seek out areas where the temperature and oxygen content are balanced, so if you want to catch them, you need to find these preferred areas.

As discussed earlier, fish have the ability to sense temperature changes to a fraction of a degree. They can pick up temperature changes from their skin receptors. Each type of trout prefers a fairly specific range of temperature within which it is comfortable. If the water is too cold, the fish become lethargic, listless, go into semihibernation, feeding very little. If the temperature is too warm, they will become overheated and resist feeding, typically moving away to try to find a cooler layer of water. The conflict for the fish is that although cooler water absorbs oxygen well, cooler water at a depth, which would be preferable, is not usually well oxygenated. Lack of contact with air at the surface and lack of vegetation at depth keep levels low, so the fish must find the right mix elsewhere.

Each species of fish also has a different tolerable temperature range within which they are able to function normally. Even within the trout family there is considerable variation on what the brook, lake, and rainbow trout prefer as a reasonable temperature. The table below gives you a feel for what these are:

TABLE 1: Preferred and ideal temperatures for trout

Trout	Low	High	Difference	Ideal
Rainbow	50	65	15	57
Brook	53	65	12	60
Lake	40	55	15	45
Brown	55	70	15	60

You can see that the lake trout is happy at around 45 degrees, which is why he likes to hang out at depths. The brook trout, on the other hand, is able to deal with a considerable range of temperatures because the stream environment is so variable. Each fish will instinctively seek his own special comfort zone. Although they may take the odd vacation, or travel through hostile waters, they will inevitably settle for their own preferred area. If they cannot, then they become inactive. As water becomes too cold, their metabolism slows, and they become listless. Fish will feed little in cool temperatures, so you will waste time fishing in water that is the wrong temperature.

Yet another factor to consider is the effect of air temperature at surface. The air has a tendency to change the temperature of the surface water. Changes in air temperature, particularly if sustained for continuous periods (even short periods, like over a half day), can result in changing the surface water enough to force fish down (during the day) or bring them up (after nightfall). As a general guide, the table below offers some clues for rainbow trout.

if air less than 50°F	fish are passive	so fish deeper
if air from 50° to 60°	fish are active	so fish near surface
if air from 60° to 70°	fish are very active	so fish near surface
if air greater than 70°	fish are passive	so fish deeper or in shade

Even on a daily basis, as air and water interact through the night, the water will be cooler in the morning, with more oxygen. The fish will be more prone to feed at surface during these times. The key point to all this is that it is senseless to fish in water that does not contain sufficient oxygen, or is not of the right temperature.

On the Water. It was 9:00 A.M. and a fantastic fall day in September. We had rushed to get out on the lake just after the wind subsided. It had been a hot summer and the fishing hadn't been great so it was time to make up for lost time. "Well, Mike, what's the prognosis today? I don't see any feeding activity—where do you suggest we start?" Mike tried desperately to appear intelligent. "Well—I'd say that fall isn't here yet and it has been relatively warm, so the thermocline must still be in place. It's 65 degrees and it was cooler through the night, so the surface has had a chance to cool a bit. The water temperature at surface is about 63, and these trout are happy at 57 degrees, so the oxygen is good at surface and there is every indication that they should be close to surface, ready to feed. Let's troll a couple of different flies just below surface. If that doesn't work, then we should go a bit deeper as the sun rises and it gets brighter."

There is nothing particularly revealing about this, except that locating the possible layer of water where the fish should be becomes a bit more predictable; knowing a few simple things about fish and temperature will help you to identify the layer. Now let's take a closer look at how temperatures change in bodies of water, depending on the season. We are going to start with summer because that is the most popular time.

It may be quite apparent by now that the difficulty for both fish and angler is to deal with this problem of shifting temperature and oxygen. The fish and the angler must solve the same problem, the fish to survive, the angler to catch the fish. To help us find these waters, there are some simple scientific principles that we need to recall. It turns out that we can, in fact, make some logical conclusions on where we can find the best water. Let's examine this more closely.

2.2 FISH IN THE SUMMER THERMOCLINE

Tactics. As summer approaches, a layer of cool water with good oxygen levels forms. This is called a thermocline. This layer provides the most suitable habitat where you are most likely to find trout.

Concepts and Application. In the last section, it was clearly noted that fish have a preference for water that has the right mix of temperature and oxygen. To an angler, it would be beneficial if there were some way of determining where such preferred water is on any body of water. But considering the changing winds, currents, temperatures, etc., is this really possible? Well, in fact, there is some rhythmic sense to this problem. We first need to understand some water dynamics. You will probably be wondering what the word *thermocline* is. A thermocline layer is a technical word for a layer of water in a stationary body of water that contains the greatest range of temperature. This thermocline is where fish will most often be found, simply because they can find two key ingredients to survival. Because this water is cooler, it will typically have a good supply of oxygen.

To understand how the overall temperature of water changes, we must look at the series of changes that lake water undergoes during a year. The best example is taken from a body

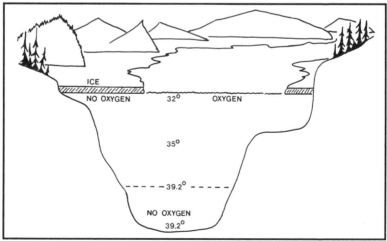

Figure 1. Lake temperature in winter

of water that goes through the most severe seasonal variations. First, let us consider what happens to a lake in the winter. Keep in the back of your mind some of the simple properties of water that we learned in the high school science lab. If you boil water, it will evaporate into the air. If we take water and cool it, it will become heaviest at 39.2 degrees Fahrenheit. (You probably forgot that little fact!) If you continue to cool it, it will get lighter and freeze at 32°F, finally turning to ice. Because it can change its weight, it actually sinks or rises, depending on its temperature. This is why ice, which is the lightest, is at the top. So, although a lake might look like it is completely still, its water is actually moving and mixing throughout the year.

Let us begin the process by looking at a typical lake and its water movements. The story opens as we move into winter and the ice starts to form on the water. The lake will look like that shown in Figure 1.

As the water becomes colder due to the cooling air temperature, it gets denser, or heavier, and gradually sinks. Water is heaviest at 39.2°F, after which it becomes increasingly less dense until it forms ice at 32 degrees. The ice will, therefore, float to the top, forming an insulating layer from the cold air above. As you will see in Figure 1, the temperature will therefore change gradationally from 32 (ice) to its maximum density of 39.2 at the

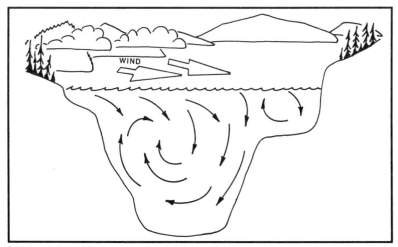

Figure 2. The spring overturning of a lake

bottom. If the lake is covered with snow, there will be poor light penetration and a poor oxygen level to support fish life, except near the top. If light can get through, then oxygen will be closer to the top, which is where the fish will have to be.

With reference to Figure 2, in the spring, when the ice starts to melt, the sun warms the surface water and the wind helps to mix the water and shift it downward. As the water warms toward 39.2, it gets heavier and starts to sink. The water at the bottom is therefore displaced and forced upward, where it can be re-oxygenated and reheated. This is known as *overturning*.

When the ice finally disappears, the fish will begin to move to the surface where it is a bit warmer. This is typically because the sun continues to warm the surface water and the sinking action will continue until the lake reaches equilibrium at the same temperature of 39.2. At this short period of time, fish can be found at any level because the whole body of water is the same temperature. As spring proceeds, the water at surface starts warming beyond 39.2 and it stops sinking. The natural tendency is to form

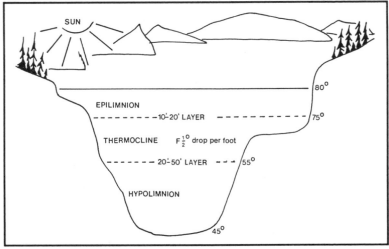

Figure 3. Lake stratification in summer

stratified layers of water temperature. As this continues, another stage of equilibrium is reached—where three distinct stratified layers are formed. This is shown in Figure 3.

The warm surface is called the *epilimnion*, while the cold bottom layer is called the *hypolimnion*. The middle layer is the one of interest, called the *thermocline*. It is the layer where the most rapid temperature change exists. By definition, the thermocline is the layer where temperature changes at least half a degree per foot of depth. Although the thickness of the layers is subject to many variables, the top and bottom rarely exhibit more than a 5-degree range. But the thermocline can change one-half degree Fahrenheit per foot, typically ranging from 75 to 55 degrees. In general, the warm layer will range from 80 to 75 degrees while the thermocline will range from 75 to 55 degrees. The bottom will once again have a narrow range below 55 degrees. But the bottom, particularly if deep, contains a poor supply of oxygen, is dark, and may be too cool, so the fish will prefer the thermocline where a better combination provides the best metabolic balance. As a rough guide, the epilimnion will be a layer from 0 to about 20 feet deep, while the thermocline will be 20 to 50 feet deep. During the summer, particularly if it is a hot one, the upper layer increases in depth, forcing the fish deeper. The lower layer loses oxygen because there is no photosynthesis to produce oxygen. So, although a state of equilibrium is reached during the early summer, the layers will change in thickness as summer progress, making fish move down farther to find the appropriate zone.

On the Water. The summer was swelteringly hot, with very little relief anywhere. The top layer of water was around 73 degrees, a far cry from the 57 degrees that the rainbow trout prefers. To anybody on the lake, it was obvious that the fish were nowhere to be seen. Interestingly enough, we could see a few boats at the far end of the lake where you could spot the odd glitter of willow leaves. So we headed down there. "How's the fishing?" asked Mike as we cruised by one of the boats.

"Pretty tough," came the reply. "I've had to go to the big hardware and worms to pick up two fish in the last four hours. I hate to admit it, but if I come in without any fish, my wife is going to laugh at me. I'll never hear the end of it. I've been here for two days dragging flies and plugs. I don't normally use these leaves but I'm desperate."

Mike was staring at the man's willow leaf, which was almost 4 feet long, obviously in disbelief that any one would stoop to an illegal leaf. I noted two large weights. "Man you must be deep with all that lead," I commented.

"Yup," the man admitted, "but I wasted two hours dragging this bloody thing around without any weight."

I finally had to kick Mike to get his attention so we could push on. "Well good luck with your wife," I said. "We might give a few plugs a try."

The fish were obviously well below surface. Most of the lake was shallow, except for the far end of the lake. This observation was reinforced by the few fish that old fellow had caught on the willow leaves. We had been told that the lake was an average of 30 feet deep, so if the thermocline was somewhere between 20 to 50 feet deep, this would not leave too much of the lake with a desirable temperature range. In fact, the long, hot summer would have forced the fish to look for deeper water. The fish would have to be down about 40 feet to get to some tolerable water temperature—about where the willow leaf was!

I told Mike, "I definitely feel that we will be wasting our time in any area but the one deep end of the lake. The other important factor in this is that the fish will prefer to keep away from the open water, so the best area would be where the thermocline is in direct contact with the steeper, protected shoreline. That area over there has a steep shoreline which looks like its water is deep, so we should troll in that area. I would like to first go over and measure how deep it is."

After measuring the depth of water at 80 feet along the shoreline, the strategy was obvious: four weights for me and five weights for Mike, 70 pulls out as a start—but no worms. We would go as deep as possible first and sweep along the bluffs. If that didn't work, we would work our way up 10 pulls at a time.

2.3   FISH NEAR SURFACE IN FALL AND SPRING

Tactics. As the season changes to fall and the air temperature starts to cool the surface water, the fish will begin to change their feeding habits and start rising closer to surface. This is a time when flies and surface fishing are the best alternatives.

Concepts and Application. Let us continue the story as we approach the fall. We last left the lake as the three layers had formed, creating a state of equilibrium. Continued heat had made the fish drop deeper as the thermocline moved lower. But as the temperature cools toward fall, the water cools at the surface and sinks, forcing lighter water up. As the water cools at the surface, the fish come to the top to feed, also finding better oxygen levels. Because there is typically a lot of insect activity in the fall, this is the best time to try flies. As the fall gets cooler, this mixing action continues, just as it did in the spring, until another state of equilibrium is reached when the water cools to 39.2. The cooling will continue until the water starts to freeze.

The above process takes us through the complete cycle, so the temperature of the water starts to look like it did in the spring. Essentially, the picture of the lake in the fall is similar to that which was shown in Figure 2. The lake goes through the overturning process when the water becomes reasonably stable throughout the lake. At this time the fish will become active throughout the lake, since the distinct layers of water become mixed up. The fish will tend to move to those areas which are richer in oxygen and food, rather than to just those that have the ideal temperature.

On the Water. It was early morning on the lake, a fantastic fall day in September. The nights were becoming cooler now and you could feel a chill lingering in the morning air. We had rushed to get out on the lake, as 2-pound rainbows were flopping on the water everywhere. Many were just rolling like miniature dolphins, obviously picking up food off the surface. We had decided to do some scientific analysis that day. It had been cool for two days and the fish had not surfaced like they were this day. For the past few days, in other words, the fishing was poor. What was happening?

Mike had bought a temperature probe which he was itching to use. When you drop this probe into the water, it provides a digital readout. "I know this is pretty silly, Ed," he said, "but I really want to verify this business of temperature shifts. Let us head out there right where those big ones are surfacing." Mike then took 10 readings at 5-foot depths. The surface water temperature was 55 degrees, then the readings were 54, 54, 52, 50, 51, 50, 49, 49, 48. The air was 45. "Well, Mike," I asked, "what's the prognosis today? They are rising everywhere; if you keep doing your analysis long enough, one of these trout will land in the boat! When do you think we can fish?"

Mike was super cool. "Well, I'd say that the thermocline must be in the process of mixing and the surface waters are quite cool. It's 45 degrees and it was cooler through the night, so the surface has had a chance to cool quite a bit. Right now, the surface layer is exactly what these rainbows prefer for optimum metabolic functioning. No wonder they are so active at the surface; it's like feast time in paradise for them. The oxygen is good at surface and the fish must love it since that's the temperature they like. Normally they won't take anything except tiny nymphs at surface when they rise like this but I would bet that they will go after flies. We should be trolling close to surface. Let's troll a couple of different flies just below surface."

Well, he was right. It was hardly 5 minutes after the Spratley was out that the silver 2-pound flash exploded out of the water.

The key point is that as the lake waters start to mix again in the fall, the fish become more active at surface, being particularly interested in the now-mature insect life. The same is true of the spring. And the water where the fish should be becomes more easily predicted. Simply knowing a few things about fish and temperature is crucial to identifying the place to fish. Now let us look at the other two survival requirements of shelter and food.

2.4   FIND STRUCTURAL SHELTERED AREAS

Tactics. The fish's basic survival instinct will be to avoid predators and conserve energy by selecting structural features that allow protection. Such areas have identifiable characteristics and should be sought out as the more preferred fishing spots.

Concepts and Application. Once fish are able to satisfy their top priority items of temperature and oxygen, they will need to take care of the next two requirements—shelter and food. Fish will select sheltered areas to protect themselves from predators and bright sunlight. They will tend to situate themselves within short distances of structures or physical situations that will offer cover. Typically these are underwater drop-offs, shorelines, ledges, overhanging trees, channels, rocks, docks, underwater vegetation, log booms, and so on. There are some key reasons for this that are based on their physiological makeup. Although we will explore this in more detail in the next chapter, let us look briefly at some key scientific facts.

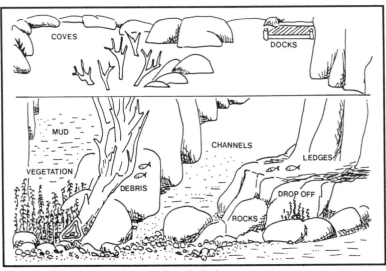

Figure 4. Fish's need for structural shelter

Fish are very conscious of the need to conserve energy because they cannot afford to expend it. This means that they are "lazy" and will seldom chase anything a long distance. In fact, fish must rest a long time if they expend effort through a burst of energy. Fatigue will set in quickly and it can take hours to recover. To give you some perspective, consider that a trout can lose 50 percent of its glycogen (roughly translated: power in muscles) only after a few minutes of heavy exertion. That means that once you tire that 2-pound fish, there is no way he can recover quickly. If he gets away after 5 or 10 minutes of fighting, he will need most of the day to recover. It can take one hour to replenish 30 percent of the lost energy, 2 hours to get to 45 percent, and 3 hours to get to 65 percent. If a fish gets too burned up, it can take a whole day to recover. The process of overexertion also creates another danger. Exertion will create a lactic acid accumulation, which causes fatigue buildup, peaking within hours. If lactic acid becomes excessive in the blood, it can stop the heart, or block oxygen to the blood. The result can be fatal, so the fish tries not to fool with this problem.

Although the rate of energy consumption will vary with the size and type of fish, there is a rule of thumb that depicts them in general. They can swim slowly, at about 5 body lengths per second, and suffer no fatigue. Or they can swim in bursts of up to 20 body lengths per second and suffer rapid fatigue. Alternatively, they can swim at a moderate speed of about 10 body lengths per second and get slow fatigue.

Fish can swim slowly, and roll in the water, moving with currents to conserve energy and not overextend themselves. Or they can go through rapid bursts, in which case the fatigue will set in within minutes. The moderately swimming fish can swim for a few hours without the onset of fatigue. Migrating fish will tend to budget their energy activities, every so many hours finding resting and feeding stations to regain energy levels. The point is that fish will prefer resting areas where they do not have to swim against currents, or they do not need to swim far for protection. They will seek areas where they do not have to spend much energy catching food. Many of these places on any body of water are quite obvious.

Eddies, for example, are formed as water moves by a point of land or some physical obstruction. The movement of water such as from a stream entering the lake will create cyclic movements of water as it passes by any land obstruction. As the current passes these barriers, it can create circular eddies of backwater where bait fish gather, thus attracting fish. The slower circulating water also attracts resting fish. The same effect is produced by

Figure 5. Eddies, pools, and land obstructions

depth changes vertically. These areas are typically a good bet to try. Such places offer fish a chance to rest, away from a current and near possible food sources, since the water here will also attract smaller fish.

As shown in Figure 5, there are other natural or man-made structures that form shelter. Typically, these are underwater drop-offs, shorelines, ledges, overhanging trees, channels, rocks, docks, underwater vegetation, or even log booms. All of these offer protective or desirable features that will attract fish.

The position of the sun is another factor that needs to be considered. Fish will avoid the brightness and will move down in the water when the sun is bright. The expression is "sun up, fish down, sun down, fish up." This will make any shade areas much more desirable to the fish, such as cliff side or mountain shadows. Similarly, on a cloudy day, the fish will be closer to surface because there is less brightness. Most fish do not like clear water or bright sunlight, so cloudy water and shaded areas are attracters. These factors should be considered in your selection of spots.

On the Water. After several hours on the lake, with limited action, we decided to take a cruise down to the far end of the lake. We had been on the water for two hours now and had netted two small fish. Pretty poor performance for our efforts, but it was quite obvious that we were just not fishing in the right place. The previous day had given us a bit of success. We had caught five beauties just off the large bay using the recommended plugs, but today there was just no significant action. Through the night, the storm must have stirred up the bay, so the fish obviously had moved, or they just were not feeding.

"Either we go in, or we seek out a new spot, Ed," Mike mumbled. "We can't go in with these two small fish; we'll never hear the end to it." So the cruise was one of visual inspection. It was now midday and the summer sun was warm. Where would we find these fish? As we cruised down the lake, we began to appreciate the beauty of the area—the mountains in the distance, the blue sky, the tranquil blue water, and the wildlife spending the day actively. "Ah, this is what life is all about, Ed. Pass me a beer—it's noon anyway." Just then we approached a new section of the lake. You could see that the lake had become shallow, with the vegetation, mostly cattails and bulrushes, invading the lakeshore. This would not do; it would be too shallow and the temperature would probably be too warm. As we continued, we could see the shoreline changing. It was becoming rocky now, with conifers hanging over the water. The water looked much deeper. As we droned farther on, we could see a rocky point in the distance. You could see a calm area just past the point, protected from the steady light breeze of midday.

"Let's head around that point, Ed; it looks interesting. If I was a fish, I would be tempted to hang out over there." As we came around the point, the sight was too much for us mortal anglers to take. A cool, dark blue bay about 2,000 feet wide was nestled in a nook of the mountain. The sun was behind the cliffs, so much of the water along the shore was in shade. Just about midway, a small estuary had forced its way into the deep water.

Just to the right, between it and the mountain, you could see a deep blue channel cut into the lake. The geological fault that had created this was evident as a cut through the mountain. "Ed, this is incredible. I've never seen a spot like this," Mike exploded in excitement as his reel hand started to shake. "Let's take a sweep past this point and cut up that channel, then sweep past the estuary around the bay and come around again. Just around this point, I would swear there is a ledge down there where the giants live."

We went deep on the first sweep—eighty pulls. Just as we came into the channel, Mike shortened his troll by ten pulls. It was about five seconds after that when the big one hit. What a fight, and what an afternoon!

2.5   FISH NEAR NATURAL FOOD SOURCES

Tactics. Fish cannot afford to expend high energy to swim for food since their energy levels can be depleted rapidly. They will therefore tend to stay close to food sources that can be identified as surface or subsurface features. Such features represent good fishing holes and should be sought out.

Concepts and Application. In conjunction with the above description on sheltered areas, it follows that fish will prefer to congregate where they can find both shelter and plentiful food sources. In any body of water, there will be a tendency for fish to seek out areas where there is a sign of other life activities because these may offer an abundance of food. In most situations, these areas can be identified quite easily by visual means. For example, streams entering the lake, overhanging rocks, weeds, brush, drop-offs, and ledges can be readily identified as features which attract fish because they offer a source of food. In many cases, the same areas that offer shelter to a trout will also offer the same facility to other fish so it is reasonable to expect that trout will stay there to feed. The point is that any feature or structure, above or below the water, that will attract fish and other edible organisms will also attract the predatory trout.

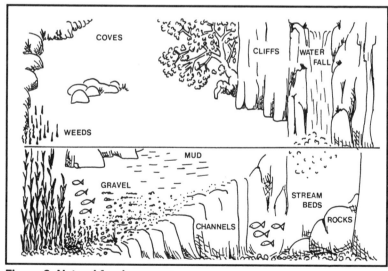

Figure 6. Natural food sources

Figure 6 shows some of the common areas that can be identified as possible sources of food for trout. You will note that many of these are also common areas of shelter. Any area that can provide both food and cover is most often the preferred location for schools of fish. It is not too difficult to pinpoint these features. Here are some of the more common, obvious ones.

Surface Features. Surface features are those that can be determined by a visual inspection of the area. Most of these are easily distinguished, including coves, overhanging trees, waterfalls, and vegetation. For example, coves and points of land offer fish a haven in that these areas typically contain less active waters or they harbor vegetation, have stream outlets, and are therefore more likely to have other life. These areas are typically protected from the elements of wind and storm, allowing various organisms to flourish. The coves, particularly if deep enough to have cooler water, will therefore attract trout.

Any place where trees or brush can be noted as hanging over the water are good areas. Surface vegetation is a crucial item in that overhanging brush and trees will create natural places that will have food drop into the water. Similarly, waterfalls or stream entry points will typically pinpoint where debris or food life can be present. This can come in the form of organisms that are washed down stream, or other organisms that like the extra oxygen. Any area where vegetation can be seen at surface, such as reeds, weeds, and brushes, will typically harbor other life forms that may be desirable to a trout. The trout may have a tendency to "cruise " these areas to pick up the odd organism.

Subsurface Features. These are features that are not readily distinguished by visual inspection. They are features that you learn to read by other signs and activities. These include underwater vegetation, mud, gravel and rock bottoms, channels, and underwater stream beds. Water vegetation is a source of oxygen as it expels it during the day from photosynthesis. This is where many other edible species are apt to stay. If the water is deep and the water temperature is cooler, the combination will act as an even better attraction. Very often a mud or gravel bottom will harbor places where various life forms can be found foraging, reproducing, or simply living out their existence. Often, the type of bottom will reveal the type of organisms that inhabit it.

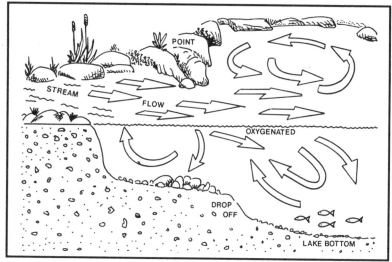

Figure 7. The stream into the lake

Stream outlets are very often good sources of food since the stream will carry various debris and food, not only attracting other life, but carrying particles of food as well. Fish will have a tendency to stick around these areas, particularly if the stream creates a channel into the body of water and is situated in a thermocline. One of the best situations is the one shown in Figure 7 where a good-sized stream (with oxygenated water) has formed a deep channel in the lake.

On the Water. We had swept most of the lake with nothing but an odd nibble—just enough to keep us trying a little longer before we gave in. It was now late in the afternoon. We had been out there for three solid hours. The sun was still high in the sky and we were getting a bit toasted. "Let's just go by that little estuary one more turn, Ed," Mike coaxed. "I am absolutely certain I had a nibble over there—and I thought I saw a boat over there with some net action." So off we went another time. But—nothing! "Mike," I said, "I think it's too shallow for a frog to do a back-stroke in this area; you probably hooked some weeds. Let's stop and check the depth." After only ten reel cranks, I hit bottom. "Well, Mike, my case rests," I crowed. Mike responded quickly. "Don't blame me, Ed, you're not exactly an encyclopedia of ideas. Maybe the fish are always hanging around creeks entering the lake—I read that in several books."

I took a few minutes on this one. "Well, if you insist, then we should go and find a real stream, not a minnow channel. Let's head down to the south end of the lake—there is a river entering there—perhaps you're right. The sun was now starting to drop behind the mountain. As we headed down the lake, you could see the river had cut a narrow gorge through the mountains, finally cascading into a large bay. You could see that the years of water movement had carved a deep dark blue channel, about fifty feet wide where it entered the main lake. The water turned a deep, dark blue, then merged into the lake as the water depth became constant. You could see slow water rolling and swirls around the cliff wall as the stream current pushed by the jutting rock bluff. "Man, how could any normal fish ignore this paradise?" Mike giggled as he rummaged through his flatfish box. "Let's swing up into the channel and cut to the right where that rock cliff is. The water looks really deep along there, and it's shady."

Need I tell the rest? This was the perfect spot. The fish could dash out into the channel from the protection of the rock bluffs and forage in the channel or pick up goodies in the back eddies. The water was deep and cool, with good oxygen close by. The ledge provided a nice shaded area. From then on, the time went fast!

2.6 USE THREE KEY TROLLING METHODS

Tactics. There are three key methods of trolling that can effectively cover all water depths. These are the surface, midwater, and bottom trolling methods. They should be selected according to the level of water sought.

Concepts and Application. Although there is a wealth of trolling techniques and setups that you can use to seek out gamefish, there are three very distinct methods that will quite adequately cover all trolling requirements. Typically you will need to fish close to surface, somewhere below surface at a constant depth, or you may want to go right to the bottom. With reference to Figure 8, the three methods are illustrated.

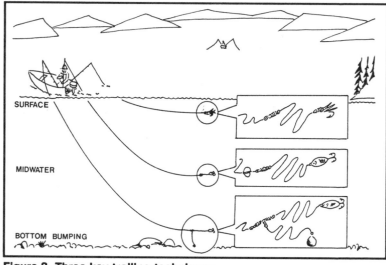

Figure 8. Three key trolling techniques

    Surface Trolling. Surface trolling is used to fish close to the surface when it is felt that the fish are feeding close to, or at, the surface. As illustrated in Figure 8, the typical setup includes dragging a fly, or a light lure or plug, along the surface at some constant speed which will cause it to simulate the movement of real bait. In this case, you will be trolling a light swivel, a length of leader line, and a fly (or equivalent). The difference with this

48

method and the other two is that you should consider a fairly long and light leader if you are planning to drag right on surface. On a calm day, dragging a line on the surface will create the illusion of a long "crack" on the surface water, which easily spooks the fish. A leader of 12 to 15 feet would not be too long in this case.

Midwater Trolling. Midwater trolling is usually what most trollers are familiar with. The common setup is the weight, swivel, leader, and bait. In this case, a specific depth below surface is sought, along with a specific type of bait action. If a willow leaf is being used, then the setup will be different (weight, snap swivel, leaf, leader, bait) as it will be for salmon (snap swivel, dodger, swivel, leader, bait). The basic plan here is to be able to control the depth at which bait is being shown to the prospective "client." The use of weights and length of line are the key elements to depth control. Speed can also be used but it is easier to keep this variable out of the picture.

Bottom Bumping. A bottom bumping technique can be used very successfully if the bottom is not covered over with logs, thick vegetation, or debris that can snag your apparatus. The typical setup is shown in Figure 8, including a 3-way swivel, a light leader to a bell sinker, and a leader from the 3-way swivel to the swivel and bait. The leader that goes to the bell sinker is the lightest (half of the main line) and the length of it will vary but 2 feet will usually suffice. The bait is therefore free to trail (2 to 6 feet) along as the bell sinker bumps its way along the bottom. If the bait has any weight to it, then you need to up the length of the bell sinker line. The bell sinker is round and smooth so it is less likely to snag. The sinker line is also the lightest so if you do get snagged then you can still pull the rest free.

On the Water. This was a totally new lake to us. We had heard about the big ones that grew to 8 pounds in this lake. The lake was big, 5 miles long and an average of 2 miles wide. The lake was shaped like a sausage, with the longer direction trending east-west. Our first "inspection trip" of the lake showed an incredible array of different features and terrain types. Swamps and weeds at one end, little islands at the south end, rock bluffs to the north, and streams entering in at least five places. The water was murky, teeming with organic life in some areas. In several spots where the streams entered the lake, they formed estuaries which jutted out into the lake. This lake was hard to read. You could not tell the depth anywhere.

"I have a feeling that we are going to lose some gear here, Ed," Mike muttered. "How do you suppose we use a process of elimination here?"

It was my chance to be clever. "Well, I think we need to get down into the thermocline in this lake, Mike, but unless we do a lake survey, we don't know how deep the lake is. I think we should hit the bottom section of the water. I am going to use the bottom-bumping technique with about 10 feet to the bell sinker and troll right down the middle. You can troll midwater with a half ounce of weight, just to get into the top part of the thermocline. You can go deeper if the lake is deep. We should get a good feel for the depth and nature of the bottom this way. If there is anything there, we will run into it."

So I let out 90 pulls before I felt the irregular motions set out by the bumps of the bell sinker. Mike let out 50 pulls and sat back in his seat, watching the bottom-bumping master at work. You could see my rod tip bend and release in a reasonably rhythmic fashion. It was about 50 feet to the bottom, which was pretty irregular. You could then see the tip bend and struggle as the weight encountered resistance. "Weeds," I mumbled. "Weeds at 40 to 50 feet means action, Mike; get the net ready." Mike was getting no action at all. "I think I will reel in and go 50 with more weight. Obviously we have depth enough to troll deeper." Just then, my rod tip started to jerk in spasms. I was right; we had found the right depth.

2.7   APPLY A DEPTH ITERATION PROCESS

Tactics. Fish will be found at different depths according to the season, the weather, and the time of day. Since their most active feeding times are usually not more than two hours, you need to seek out the active feeding layer as quickly as possible.

Concepts and Application. It is quite commonly accepted that fish will typically feed close to the surface at dawn and at dusk, then they will vary their feeding depth between 0 and 100 feet at other times of the day. This aspect was dealt with in the section on water temperature and the need for oxygen. This fact will also become more apparent in the *what* chapter, where some of the physiological and sensory aspects are discussed. Essentially, however, the variable-level feeding problem means that to avoid wasting time fishing at the wrong depth, you must always be aware of ways to find the fish at the right depth. Secondly, because the fish do not feed actively for extended periods of more that a few hours, you need to find them as fast as possible.

First, you must recall the "pull" and "handle" methods to keep control of distance. As discussed in the chapter on fundamentals, one of the simplest ways to measure line distance is the "pull" method, where you grasp the line at the reel and pull out an "arm's length" of line, thereby releasing about 1.5 feet into the water, or whatever length your arm measures. You can easily keep track of the amount of line being let out this way. Either this or the handle method is useful to measure the horizontal distance of the line as you let it out when trolling. The key, however, is that you need to use some method to be effective. By applying this technique, you are indirectly seeking the right depth.

As you read more about the habits of fish, you will realize that there are many reasons why the fish will not seek out the bait. He basically relies on you to find him, or to maneuver your bait to within a certain proximity so that he can use smell, sight, sound, or vibration to hone in on his target. Finding fish still relies on your ability to seek out the right combination of bait, speed, setup, and depth, even if you are in a hot area. Remember the process of elimination? This process must be activated quickly and the best way is to troll several lines. If you have two or three lines, troll 3 different weights at the same distance for

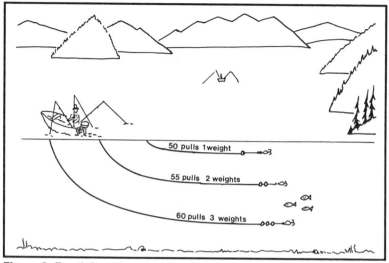

Figure 9. Depth iteration process

about 10 minutes. Then let out another 20 feet and troll for 10 more minutes; or change the bait type. The key resides in working your depths, techniques, and bait to quickly find the right combination and, of course, eliminate the wrong combinations. If action is slow or nonexistent, troll another combination until you find the right depth and bait. The key is to remember the pulls and the weight so that the successful formula can be replicated. This tactic may help find the optimum combination for that specific time.

Speed is another way to control the depth but the usual trolling kicker is not so accommodating when it comes to being specific about speed. The easiest way is to keep your speed constant once you are happy with the action of the bait. If you want to have an idea how fast you are moving, drop a floating object at the front end of the boat and count the seconds for it to reach the back end of the boat. Five seconds to get to the back of a 15-foot boat will give you 3 feet per second, so you can check this easily. In rough water, or when trolling upwind, you can hang a bell sinker on 2 feet of line from your boat into the water. Note the angle as you troll at your desired speed. You can adjust the speed of the boat to attain this same angle. If, for example, you are trolling upwind and the same motor speed does not result in the proper angle, then you would increase the speed to adjust.

Another thing to consider is that you should try to keep the line from going out too far. More than 150 feet is excessive. Longer line with the same weight only drops the lure slightly lower due to increased line resistance with water. Additionally, the longer line has a greater chance of tangling with other lines. Yet another disadvantage of extra length is that the fish becomes needlessly far away from the boat, lessening your control of the situation.

The key to depth control resides in how you change weights and the length of line. Since you never know exactly where the fish are, you need to try alternative depths to find them. Once you have a nibble, if you have kept track of the weight and the line out, it becomes a simple matter to reproduce the successful combination and go over the same water. In this way, you never really have to know exactly what the true vertical depth is, or at what depth the fish are feeding; you only need to know the line distance. At the same speed, you only have to know the weight and the line length (pulls) out to be at the right place. So you don't have to carry a calculator and be a mathematician to figure depth. As a rough rule of thumb, you can consider that for every foot of vertical depth, you will need to let out 5 feet of line (average trout setup). So if you want to drop to 20 feet, you need 100 feet of line.

On the Water. It was already approaching 10:00 A.M. when we hit the water. The wind had subsided and the sun was struggling to find its way through the cloud cover. Like most storms in the high country, it brought a quiet, fresh period when the air is clean and the water still. You could feel the fish needing to feed; after all, the storm had started some 20 hours ago and those fish had to be hungry. We had to find them fast. We had a feeling that, when the feeding started, it would be fast and furious. At 10:15, we could see the odd swirl as a riser cruised the surface for insects. It was time to try our hottest flatfish. Mike had a plan. "OK, Ed, this weather has screwed everything up for these fish, and they could be at any depth, so we are going to iterate as fast as possible. Why don't you try an orange one? Since it's still cool, my guess is that they are in the top 20 feet, so I am going to troll with 2 weights and 50 pulls. Why don't you go for 50 pulls and 1 weight, Ed? We had some good action over there yesterday so let's troll along that shoreline."

After 10 minutes of trolling and no action, I said, "Mike, I'm going down deeper with 3 weights."

"OK," Mike said, "I'll go 10 more pulls but I am going to change to a blue and red, then head toward that bay over there."

After 10 more minutes, and still no action, I said: "Well, I think we should take a sweep around the bay one more time. There is no action at these depths on this flatfish, and they are rising, so I am going back up to top with a Spratley." After 50 pulls and 10 minutes, I felt a nibble on the line. "Mike, I just had a nibbler back there. I think we should take another sweep over that area and you should come back up close to surface with your flatfish."

"OK," he said, "I'll go for one weight and 60 pulls."

After about 5 minutes into the sweep over the same area, Mike's rod showed a quick jerk, followed by a silver flash about 75 feet back as the trout rose to surface trying to spit the plug. After some intense action, the 20-inch trout was in the net. "Congratulations Mike, blue and red, 60 pulls and one weight, right? Let's go over the same area—you got any more blue and reds?"

I was just at 55 pulls when the next one hit. It had taken 35 minutes to find these fish. This intoxicating session lasted for another two hours, then it stopped as quickly as it had started. It didn't matter, however, as we had our limits—and our excitement.

The process of depth iteration was being used to find the fish, by trying different depths and different bait. Once we felt a nibble, the fertile area became more specific. Once we made a strike, the rest was obvious. We made some mistakes, but the process of elimination worked to get to the target. We had figured out the right depth in 35 minutes.

2.8   CHECK OUT THE LAKE WATER TYPE

Tactics. There are many bodies of water that are hostile to organic food in that they are acidic and cannot support fish life. These lakes can be identified by certain characteristics so you should not waste time fishing them.

Concepts and Application. When it comes to classifying lakes by their degree of fishing productivity, there are three main types. They are *eutrophic* (highly productive), *oligotrophic* (not very productive), and *dystrophic* (not productive). This classification simply relates to the amount of food in the lake and how the food chain is supported. If you look closely at a food chain in a lake, you will realize that there is a feeding hierarchy where each larger animal depends on finding smaller edible organisms to feed on. At the bottom of this sequence is the primary food source of the smaller animals, mainly algae. So algae is the primary food of these smaller organisms, which in turn are eaten by the larger animals such as shrimp larvae and snails, and these are in turn eaten by trout. Thus the basic food in all water being algae, the more algae there is in the lake the more fish you will get because the food chain is highly active and productive. Algae is visible only by the color of the water, so the color of the water is quite often a good indication of the classification of the lake— and its degree of fishing productivity.

If we look closer at what supports algae, we find that the two most important factors are oxygen and calcium. Acidic water has low oxygen and will provide a poor habitat because it does not promote growth of weeds and vegetation that will, in turn, provide an ideal environment for many forms of organic life. The green plants that require oxygen are absent so they cannot add to the supply of food, nor the supply of oxygen. Fish need to feed on the animals and insects that inhabit weeds and organic mud, where you find the larger larvae, snails, shrimp, mollusks, and so on. If these are not abundant, then the fish will resort to eating small fish, including their own kind, reducing their own numbers.

The most productive lakes are the *eutrophic* lakes which are discolored with algae. They are characteristically alkaline, with a Ph of 7.1 and greater. They are also rather shallow. Because they usually harbor abundant insect life, there is a constant depositing of organic materials from the surface, providing plentiful bottom feed in the form of organic mud. This is also a good rooting area for plants, as well as a good place to harbor other life forms such as worms, snails, larvae, all of which will attract the fish. The water will be discolored from the algae, being darker in appearance, making it difficult to see the bottom, even if you are close to shore.

The *oligotrophic* lakes are either neutral, or slightly acidic (Ph 6.9 to 7.0). They are deeper in places and are likely to have much of the shoreline dropping deeply and abruptly into deep water. Weed beds will be scattered in small areas because the acidity and the scarcity of oxygen at depth prevents their growth. Such lakes are therefore limited in food and cover. The water will be clearer, indicating that there is much less algae to support the chain.

The least productive *dystrophic* lake has a Ph of less than 6.9 and will have a bare rock or sterile peat bottom, being hostile to growth of any sort. They are acidic, deep, with long lengths of sheer rock cliffs along the shore. There will be no oxygen and the water will be clear with no algae available in any form. The least productive lake may therefore be the one that may look the best, or at least be the most picturesque. It clearly will not support the life that allows the trout food chain to exist, however.

So, the best-looking lake, with the clearest-looking water, may not be the best for trout fishing. If the lake has little vegetation, clear water, clean rocks and gravel, or steep rock walls, you may want to ask the locals about the productivity before you spend too much time trolling.

On the Water. We had been driving for several hours. It was time for a pit stop along the highway. As we drove through the mountains, the highway wound itself like a giant snake through the wilderness, making its way through the valley. As we came through the pass, we could see a long, narrow lake in the distance. The lake glittered through the trees, sparkling its emerald-blue waters like a jewel in the lush forest. As we approached the end of the lake, we could see a long shoreline of cliffs on the distant side. The highway followed the shoreline on our side, offering many parklike settings in the forest where one could reach the rocky shoreline of the lake. "What a fantastic looking lake!"

Mike gasped. "I've never seen clear blue water like that before. There must be enormous lake trout in that lake. Let's pull off here for a pit stop and put the boat in."

As we pulled off the road and headed toward the lake, you could see a rocky shoreline following the main road. We continued to drive a short distance to a gravel beach, nestled in the trees, offering us a nice area to launch the boat. There was not a person to be seen. "Man, I can't believe this—there is not a soul here—this is too good to be true, Ed." After getting out of the truck, we walked over to water's edge. You could see the water depth drop rapidly from the shoreline. The bottom could be seen for at least forty feet. As we slipped the boat into the water, you could see the bottom through the crystal clear water. "These fish should be able to see our plugs for miles in this water," said Mike. "This is going to be brutal."

We fished up and down the shorelines for two hours. We tried numerous depths, and we tried everything in the fishing box, even the willow leaf. Not even a nibble. All we could get was fantastic scenery. Finally, I could see Mike losing interest. "This is ridiculous, Ed, let's go in. I've had enough scenery." As we putted in, another truck pulled up to the shoreline. This rather official-looking gentleman got out of the truck—the local game warden. As we got out of the boat, the warden came down to greet us. "Howdy gents. How's the fishin'?" He had a strange look on his face, as if he was laughing at us. "I don't think there are any fish in this lake," I said. "We've been out there three bloody hours."

The warden peered at us from under the brim of his hat. He had obviously noticed the Vancouver license plates on our truck, and it was a chance to tell the two city slickers about fish ecology. "Well, I'll tell ya fellas, this here lake is what scientists would call acidic. It ain't never had no fish in it 'cause there ain't nothin' to eat—that's why it's so pretty and blue. There just ain't much that can grow in these rocky shores, and so nothin' will allow algae to grow. Guess to you fellas in the city, it would be like fishin' in your swimmin' pools—har, har, har! You shoulda brought your pH kits from your jacuzzi—har, har, har!"

Mike and I couldn't leave fast enough.

2.9   ASK SOME LOCAL QUESTIONS

Tactics. Local facilities, services, and fishing activities are typically focused on the local fishing knowledge. This can be attained by simply asking some key questions on when, where, and what.

Concepts and Application. Without a doubt, the quickest way to get information is to ask the appropriate people around the area. Let's face it, you are constantly on an information quest to find those elusive trout so why not use a few shortcuts to help expedite the process of elimination? If, for example, you have decided to choose a new area to fish in, you may find this simple tactic very effective to avoid wasting time. Any fishing area abounds with useful information. Here are a few suggestions on where reasonable sources of information can be found.

Fishing Activity. There is almost an uncanny telepathic process that gathers fish boats to a productive hot spot. The odd thing is that, although many fishermen go out to enjoy the outdoors and a bit of seclusion, they seem to end up gathering around the same areas, as if they were looking for a social occasion. Time after time, boats will suddenly seem to appear from nowhere when you have a fish in your net. Head for these areas.

Fishermen. With few exceptions, anglers love to boast about their catch and they are seldom shy about telling you what they used, how deep they fished, what speed was used, and even the complete rigging used to catch the prize. Ask them. It is the quickest way to get to the fish without wasting time.

Cleaning Tables. If you are at a fishing camp or a facility where there is a fish cleaning table, you will inevitably see a beaming angler displaying his catch. He is usually waiting for someone to walk by to congratulate him. Don't be shy about going over to do just that. He will be proud to tell you all the details of how he found these beauties, and what he used to catch them. Ask him. When, where, and how. You may even get a look at the fish's stomach to see what he prefers to eat. Find something in your box that resembles it.

Lodge People. If you are at a lodge or fish camp, the proprietors, owners, or resident fishing guides, or hired hands, are all usually interested in serving you to keep your business. They are keen to tell you what will work and what has worked in the area.

They want you to stay, to enjoy the place, use their services—and come back next year—so they are very willing to provide you with current information on where, when, and how. Take advantage of this offer.

Sport Shops. These people will also offer advice on what will work, so they can sell you some lures. Typically, these sources may not be as reliable, but they may be useful.

Many other examples exist and the list could go on but the main point is that you should not be shy to ask questions.

On the Water. After a long, hard drive, we finally arrived at the little town south of the famous lake which Mike had heard about from the guys at the office. They said that this lake was filled with some of the most aggressive rainbows on the continent. We booked the cabin for the June weekend and we were anxious to head up the hill to the lake. Mike said we needed some beer plus some local dry flies, and the girls needed a pit stop, so we decided to stop in the one-horse town and wander over to the small sport shop. Mike was immediately attracted to a wall full of glittering, colored lures. "Howdy," Mike said to the proprietor. "We are just heading up to the lake for a few days—what do you suggest for this time of year?" The old gentleman grabbed the cue: "Well, son, I'll tell you the real facts—these pink-and-blue wobblers have been catching monsters! It's only five bucks." Mike had been through this routine before. "Have you caught any with it?" asked Mike. "Well, no, but I heard it was great from some of the guys in the pub—oh, yes—these flatfish over here seem to be the most popular—I can't keep my stock up. The number 4 blue has been reported to be good, and this little special fly is made by the local expert—highly recommended for action." Mike and I bought a couple of each and headed for the booze shop.

After stocking the car with beer and collecting the girls, we took a short drive up the hill. We finally stopped at the lodge to check in. You could see the lake through the trees—it looked like a mirror. Mike was starting to shake with excitement—his reel hand was starting to tremble. "Man, I can hardly wait to get the line into the water." Upon arrival, we walked into the office to greet the proprietress. The wall was dotted with pictures of fish. Some fishing gear and various plugs hung randomly on the wall. After signing in and exchanging some trivial information, Mike decided to start iterating. "Well, what's the hot area and what do you recommend we try today? We've heard about the monsters living in this lake." Seizing upon the opportunity to boast about how the big ones were biting, the friendly lady began her speech:

"Well the couple in Cabin 5 went out this morning and caught 5 beauties down at the south end of the lake on a willow leaf and worm. One of the fish measured in at 20 inches. The guy in Cabin 2 said worms are smelly, so he has been trolling a number 4 blue-and-red flatfish. He brought in 3 big ones around noon, but he was fishing along the east shoreline."

Mike had heard enough. "Boy that sounds fantastic. Have you got any of those flatfish?"

"Why of course," she replied. "I also have the willow leaf— do you want one of those too?"

On the way out, we headed down to the cabin. Along the way, Mike's eagle eyes noted activity at the fish cleaning table. A happy angler was whistling away as he carefully fillet his prize. As we approached, we could see 4 beauties on the table. "Wow!" Mike gasped. "What a catch. Where did you catch these?"

"Well," the fellow replied smugly, "this big one was brought in on a blue-and-red flatfish. I've never used one so don't ask me why—the lady said it would work so I just thought I'd try it. Am I ever glad I did—I fought this monster for 15 minutes!"

"You must have gone deep," Mike prompted.

"No, not really, I had 2 little bead sinkers, probably a third of an ounce, and I was dragging about 100 feet of line when he hit. You should have seen him dance on the water! It was just out there where the rock bluffs dive into the water, at about 8:00 A.M."

By now Mike had enough information for the kill. It was time to go unpack the car. The girls were standing at the cabin looking a bit irritated.

"Man, do I ever envy you," Mike was saying, "hope we get the same luck. What about the others?"

"Oh these? I got them on a willow leaf out in the middle of the channel this morning."

By now Mike's lips were trembling and the twitch had developed on his reel hand. We thanked the gentleman and bade him farewell. "Thanks for the info. I'm going to try that flatfish and head out—see you later."

Well this sort of simple little exchange will save you a lot of hours guessing on the place and the lures. The communications are simple, friendly, and helpful. You would have offered the information in the same way. The opportunity to apply an elimination process that takes some of the trial and error out of the process is always around you.

3   WHAT DO I FISH WITH?

Now we come to the big question. Now that I know how to identify the best places, what do I fish with? This simple question has perplexed anglers for a long time. I would really hate to accumulate the number of hours that we have dragged the wrong things in the wrong place, at the wrong time. I think that of all that wrong times, most of it has been wasted trying to tantalize fish with the wrong type of bait. Quite frankly, this is because we paid more attention to what we *thought* the fish would like than to what the fish was really interested in. The key to understanding what the fish is interested in is reflected in the fish's dining needs. This obviously resides in an understanding of the fish's physiological makeup, what it eats, and how it finds meals. It would therefore make sense to understand a bit about the fish and its natural instincts.

The fish may seem to be a very simple organism but it is actually in possession of a very sophisticated set of sensing and tracking abilities that serve to help it survive. This is essentially the topic of this chapter. Knowing the physiological capabilities of the fish and some simple behavioral facts are useful when you are deciding what to fish with; such information serves you in your quest to understand your quarry. In Chapter Two we reviewed the fish's survival requirements, covering key instincts and needs. Let us elaborate.

Fish are designed to seek out and find food. They have at their disposal several very effective means for doing this— sight, smell, taste, hearing, and sensing. These abilities can be used together or independently and provide the fish with a very effective arsenal of devices to locate food or avoid dangerous situations. Most of us consider a fish to be a very simple animal, giving it little credit for any superior capabilities, yet the fish possesses some acute sensory capabilities that are superior to ours.

For example, although the fish's vision is typically not able to deal with long distances, and is thus notably used for short range, the other senses are quite acute and able to deal with more long-range locating challenges. In addition, they see very well at night. Their seeing ability is actually highly developed, allowing them to switch from night vision to day vision, although there is an adjustment period when the change occurs. In addition, scientific studies confirm that trout can distinguish many colors. If you look at their sense of smell, they are able to pick up minute molecules from major distances away and also distinguish what they are! They have been noted for picking up a smell of man from a lure. And they are able to hear extremely well, having such a highly developed sense that they have been known to hear a worm crawling along the bottom. They also have what is known as a lateral line, on each side of their bodies, which is able to sense minute vibrations over some considerable distance. They can feel very small changes in temperature, too. Fish have a tasting capability that is superior; it is as highly developed as is their means of honing in on prey. But the most incredible capability of fish is that they can use all of these capabilities to discriminate between bad and good situations—and to store these in their memories. A fish can use these capabilities to hone in on a target without even seeing it. They can even strike at it by locating it by smell, sound, or through its vibrations. Their capabilities overlap and complement each other, covering long-range to short-range detection and "locational" sensing in even the most adverse conditions.

So if you feel that the fish is poorly equipped, you are indeed misinformed. If you think about this for a minute, you soon come to realize why fish may be difficult to fool. Without a doubt, any angler who understands these capabilities is in a solid position to launch an offensive strategy to catch the fish. This all assists you in dealing with the *what* question. There is no doubt that by knowing more about these abilities, you can work them to your advantage. In the following sections, we will explore these capabilities one by one to get a better understanding of what you should use to increase your chance of catching that fish.

3.1 USE SILHOUETTE FISHING IN LOW LIGHT

Tactics. Fish have a highly adaptive seeing ability that allows them to switch to acute black and white night vision, providing highly sensitive abilities during semidarkness. Fishing at these times can be highly productive—by choosing bait as a recognizable black or gray-tone silhouette against the sky.

Concepts and Application. Fish have a highly developed ability to see. Sight is essentially a short-range sensory device in a fish. A most interesting aspect of their vision is the way they can switch from day to night vision. The fish eye contains rods for night vision (like a cat) and cones for day vision. The cones are the color receptors for day vision, sensitive to bright light. The rods are sensitive to dim light, able to allow "seeing in the dark." Humans also have rods and cones but fish have many more rods for super light-sensitive sight at night. The rods, which are about 30 times more sensitive than cones, are only capable of black and white vision, but they are very capable of seeing in dimly lit water at night or at great depths.

   The fish has another most unusual vision ability. It can switch from day vision to night vision automatically. For example, as the brightness of day fades into dusk, the rods automatically start moving to the surface of the retina, where they will stay for about two hours. This process, which is initially triggered by a setting sun, may take a few hours before the rods are operating at full capacity. As they slowly shift into position, close to the retina surface, they begin to provide enhanced ability to see in the dark for several hours. After that, the rods start to slowly retract back to their recessive positions away from the retina. The odd thing about this is that the fish brain remembers how long it is from sundown to sunup so that the cones are ready and able to see light and color at dawn. For example, if the sun sets at 6:00 P.M., the fish would have switched to full night vision by 8:00 P.M. At 10:00 P.M., after two hours of keen vision, the process starts to reverse in preparation for morning. This phenomenon appears to take place in preparation for morning-light feeding. Lake trout appear to have much better abilities to see at greater depths than rainbows, being able to distinguish certain colors at depth. Where fish have a tendency to stay at depth for extended periods, the rods will be extended continuously to provide good vision.

During the evening, just before total dark, when the rods give fish excellent vision, they are likely to change their feeding habits. Because the rods do not distinguish color, fish will go after hatches of insects on the surface, or after other bait just below surface—and with an acute accuracy. They will typically not go after anything unless it appears as a recognizable silhouette against the darkening sky, so color is of no significance. If the moon rises, then the acute vision will continue. They can stalk their food very efficiently in marginal light. At night you may even get some continued feeding activities, particularly if the sky has any light in contrast with the dark water, but, typically, the feeding will slow down during heavy darkness, to be reactivated again in the morning light.

To a fisherman, this means that the two hours before absolute darkness can be very productive for fishing. You may have wondered why many anglers stay out after dark. You may have been quite bewildered by the many fly fishermen who come out when the water is like glass and you are heading in because it is too dark. Well, they are trying their luck at matching the size and shape of a recognizable insect with a fly silhouette. At this time, color, as noted, is irrelevant. As an aside, you should note, too, that because of the sensitivity to light at night, a fish can easily be blinded by a bright light. A flashlight can therefore make fish panic, or stun them into a hypnotic trance, just as you do when someone wakes you from a deep sleep with a bright light.

The trout has another unique seeing ability. Trout are essentially near-sighted because the lenses on their eyes are round. A round lens is used for short vision (less than thirty-five feet), while a flat lens is used for long vision (far sighted). To compensate for this seemingly limiting ability to see close objects well, fish have evolved a unique process that allows them to move the lens closer to the retina, creating the same effect that a flat lens does. This is a very clever transformation that can actually give them far-sighted ability. The real uniqueness of this process is that they can actually do this to gain a simultaneous bifocal vision. Nevertheless, the far-sighted vision is not that great, so they must rely on other senses to locate food. This limitation is really not a severe handicap since the fish can probably see as well as we can underwater. The common problem to all underwater vision is that because water has a tendency to diffuse light, meaning that it scatters the light quickly, it becomes difficult to make anything out clearly beyond certain distances. As a matter of fact, it is unlikely that anyone can see even the largest object more than 100 feet away.

To summarize, the key information to a fisherman is that fish are short sighted, able to see well up to thirty-five feet, but because of their unique design, they can adjust their eyes to simultaneous bifocal vision. They also have the ability to switch to night vision, developing acute black-and-white vision which can accurately distinguish silhouettes in marginal light.

On the Water. We had been fishing most of the evening with little success. It was a pleasant enough evening, with a slight breeze skimming the water, creating patches of ripples here and there. The coolness of the evening was beginning to chill the bones. The sun was now down and dusk was slowly consuming the light of the day. The girls were getting restless. They had tucked their books away.

"Well folks," Mike yawned, "it's time to head in for the day. Let's reel in and head for the cabin; a nice glass of port by the fire would be my choice right now." It was getting dark, but the sky was light enough to see silhouettes of the landscape above the dark water. You could hear the loons shrill across the lake. Three boats were sitting still in the lagoon just over to our left side. You could just barely make out the image of fishermen standing up in their boats, and you could hear the familiar sound of fly reels breaking the evening silence. "Ed, these guys are fly fishing! I've read about these fish and their seeing ability that changes at night. It's pretty dark—I wonder if they can see a fly being trolled?" Just then a faint plop was heard behind us. The ripples in the water could be seen as the lighter sky reflected off the wave pattern. "Man, they've started to surface, Ed. We can't go in now—they are coming up for the flies that show as silhouettes against the sky. Let's just troll a tom thumb on the water, really slow."

You could hear the girls sigh in discontent. "Just how do you expect to tie a fly on in the dark, Mike?" Hope asked. "You can't even see your rod." But Mike was not one to be thwarted easily. Out came his special little flashlight. "Hold this while I find the right fly," he giggled.

The moon was now above the mountain behind us. It was indeed a remarkable evening. All around us you could hear the fish rising. You could see the ripples as they rolled into the surface water. Mike had the fly on in a flash, and out the line went. "OK, let's cruise along this shoreline," he said. We sat quietly as the boat skimmed across the dark, still water. Just as I was about to side with the girls and tell Mike to stop fooling around, Mike let out a squeal of significant volume. It was quickly followed by the scream of the reel. Well, what can I say?—it was big and it was really dark by the time we brought him in. But the best comedy was the netting action in the moonlight; it was something we remembered for some time after.

3.2 VARY LURE COLOR BY LIGHTING

Tactics. Although fish see color well in bright light, the clarity of water, water depth, and light intensity will all have a dramatic effect on what colors the fish actually sees. The lure color must compensate for such effects or the fish may not recognize the bait.

Concepts and Application. In the previous section we mentioned that trout have the ability to distinguish color—probably as good an ability as our own. This means that a fish will identify potential food on the basis of color in addition to its shape and size. Although the trout has good color vision, he must deal with a problem that is not one of his own doing, but is due to science. This relates to how color is absorbed by water. Fish begin to lose the capability to distinguish certain colors not because of their seeing ability but because of what water does to light. At night, color simply disappears and the fish sees in black and white. During the day, what the fish sees will depend upon the clarity of water and the depth of the water from where the fish is viewing the object.

In clear water, for example, almost all light, or about 99 percent of it, is gone at about 30 feet below surface. By 40 feet, all light is gone. Water clarity, or turbidity, has an even more dramatic filtering effect on light. If the water is murky, all the light can disappear within 10 feet of surface. Needless to say, if

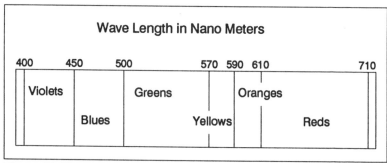

Figure 10. The color spectrum

there is very little light, then not only will it be difficult to see color, but it also will be difficult to see at all. Nevertheless,

68

because of their superior "rod seeing ability," fish require very little light to see well and can see well enough to feed at depths where the light is supposedly gone.

If you can once again remember your high school science, you will recall that the normal white light we see contains all the different colors. The color you see on an object is the one that is reflected to your eye; the others are absorbed by the object. Similarly, color is actually absorbed by the water, some colors faster than others, leaving the rest for you to see. If you look at a rainbow (the colors in normal white light), you will see how color changes by shades starting with violets, blues, then greens, yellows, oranges, and reds in a predictable fashion, as shown in Figure 10. Each color has a specific wavelength. The reds are the longer wavelengths. Wavelengths then get shorter as the colors change toward the blues. Water has a tendency to absorb the longest wavelength colors the fastest; as normal light, which contains all colors, tries to penetrate deeper, the reds become diffused quickly—within 30 feet. The next ones to disappear are orange, then yellow and so on. The shorter the wavelength, the deeper the color remains a color, simply because less is absorbed by the water. The blues can therefore be seen clearly at greater depths while the reds will just appear as a dark shade of gray. This absorbing process will have a tendency to alter the color characteristics of light below surface. It has a rather dramatic effect on what colors are actually seen by the fish at the various depths. Water absorbs reds the fastest so that by 30 feet red cannot be seen. Blues and greens are the slowest to be absorbed. A bright red lure would be bright red at surface but at 20 feet a pure red lure would not reflect reds and would appear as colorless black. If the lure was blue, then it would appear blue to the fish even at 30 feet. But if you had a lure that was a mixed blue and red at surface, the red would begin to change into a gray tone as it went deeper, finally appearing black. The resulting "mix" would be a blue-gray, moving to a blue-black, creating a much different color than you would expect. (You may have expected the blue and red to make purple. Wrong!) To get a better perspective on the color absorption process on some primary colors, have a look at Figure 11 below.

This chart will give you a good idea of what happens to the

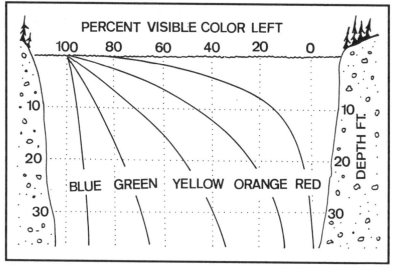

Figure 11. Color penetration and visibility by depth

primary colors as they are viewed somewhere below surface. If you are a diver, you will already know this. Note that although blues and greens last the longest, being visible beyond 100 feet, or even more in clear water, there is a depth at which everything appears blue anyway. This is so because the light isn't there at all. In this situation, a blue plug will not show up as it will blend in with the blue surroundings. So there is not much sense in thinking that a nice red plug will be seen as red 15 feet below surface. On the contrary, it will only be seen as a dark shade of gray.

Now let us add another complication. If there is a high concentration of suspended matter in the water, the whole process is reversed. The blues go first and the reds last! This process is most evident in waters that are discolored from pollution. When this is the case, you would need to use reds and yellows to show off your lure. In areas with such pollution and crap in the water, it is unlikely that you'll want to fish anyway!

To you as an angler, you just need to keep in mind that as depth, darkness, and water cloudiness increase, so will the tendency to lose the red end of the color spectrum. Essentially, these all relate to the light intensity. For example, consider the increasing darkness (at dusk) and increasing light (at dawn): at dusk the reds disappear the fastest and at dawn the blue-greens are the first to be seen. As you go deeper, you also see the reds disappear the fastest, leaving the blue-greens to be visible. As water clarity increases, this process simply accelerates. So if you want to show color, and the color that you are displaying is supposed to be recognized by the fish, then be aware of the depth, water clarity, and the color before wasting too much time. Those dazzling lures lose their dazzle very quickly in water.

On the Water. The situation was typical for someone who wasn't an angler. We had decided to take our mother out with us for a troll across the lake. She was really quite keen about the idea of coming up to do some fishing with us, so keen that she had gone to the local sport shop to buy some lures. She thought that it would be a surprise for us and also that it would be a nice gesture on her part. So she took her little bag of goodies with her on the launching raft, clutching it as she got into the boat. I started the motor and off we went to the hot end of the lake. We picked a time that we knew was going to be good, to thrill our old mom for sure. Mike picked up the rod and said, "Well, Mom, what do you think you should use to catch these trout?"

That was the perfect cue for our old trooper. "Mike, I bought some stuff back in Vancouver; this really nice fellow told me what I should buy for trout. Here they are in this bag." Mike glanced at me with a peculiar grin as he took the bag and proceeded to dump the contents on the floor. "Wow," Mike snorted, "I haven't seen stuff like this for years!" The colors were bizarre; there were color mixtures that would give a van Gogh a headache. Mike started to laugh, and I couldn't contain myself, either. "Mom, that was really nice of you but I don't think these fish have ever seen stuff like this. Are you sure you want to try these?" As she sneered right back at Mike, she picked up a flatfish that looked like a Christmas candy cane. "The nice man said this one would catch big ones—it cost me eight dollars!" "OK! OK! Let's put it on and try it." Mike knew he was treading on dangerous ground. I just quietly put on my blue flatfish and three weights, letting my line out as silently as possible. "Ed," she said, "do you want to try one?" I was quick to respond, "No thanks, Mom, I already have my line out."

The fact was that we had been relatively successful by fishing at about twenty feet below surface, where the reds, oranges, and yellows had almost disappeared. At that depth, the greens and blues would show up the best, and anything else would just show as gray tones so it was useless to try anything else. In fact, the water was fairly turbid with algae so my guess was that the red to yellow colors were gone within five to ten feet. To me, the key was more in showing these fish a clear shape of the bait in a recognizable color, mainly green. Well, I caught three fish before she asked me what I was using. We tried to explain to her how the fish would probably dart away from her lures because they wouldn't recognize what they were. On the fourth fish, she finally asked if she could use my rod. We quietly hid her bag of goodies under the seat.

3.3   AVOID FOREIGN SMELLS

Tactics. Fish can smell minute odors, which will alert them of danger, even before the bait is taken. Smell is also a primary means of recognizing and finding food. To be effective in fishing, you must not create foreign smells which will alert fish of danger.

Concepts and Application. The next acute ability that the fish has is smell. Smell is a long-distance sensing device to fish, a highly developed ability which they use to great effect to smell food or danger. Fish nostrils contain highly sensitive apparatus that can detect incredibly minute particles in the water as they pass over the sensing organs. It is reported that this is how migrating fish are able to "smell" out their place of birth. Scientific studies point to the idea that the individual fish birthplace has a combination of odors which becomes imprinted on the brain. When the fish returns years later, he essentially hones in on recognizable smells that lead him back to his origins. Apparently these fish noses are quite capable of smelling minute traces that even many scientific instruments are incapable of detecting, so they are able to smell their way back home. From an angler's perspective, this acute smelling ability is not one to be treated without respect.

The interesting part of many studies done on this topic is that the fish also *does have* this ability to memorize minute combinations of odors, as they appear to do in the case of migration. The ramification is that this capability gives a fish the ability to discriminate between odors, and identify what they belong to. In fact, fish can identify several hundreds of odors. This makes it possible for the fish to discriminate between predators, types of food, other fish, soil or mud types, types of vegetation, males or females, and probably a wide variety of things that we are not even aware of, let alone believe. In many tests conducted, it has even been concluded that fish are even able to smell distress or danger.

What this all means is that the ability of the fish to smell and discriminate among so many different situations makes it difficult to fool them. In addition, since this is a long-range sensing device, they are able to detect and avoid hostile situations well in advance. The fish may reject a plug that has no familiar odor, or it will shy away from the odor of dead fish, or even man's touch.

73

Something as harmless as handling the lure may be picked up by the fish and be immediately recognized as a foreign smell. And when you are trolling, you will be leaving a "trail of odor" behind you for the fish to pick up. On the other hand, a recognizable smell can be detected at long distances away, so this can work to your favor. Since the fish relies heavily on smell to seek out familiar food, offering live bait of a familiar variety, or artificial bait with a familiar odor, may be the most effective fishing tactic.

On the Water. I was having a great time hauling in fish. Now I was letting the small ones (less than two pounds) go. Mike was using the identical lure, the same weight, and he was trolling at the same depth. Yet after an hour he was not even getting a nibble. "I've seen this before," Mike said, "I must be sending these fish some bad vibes—what the hell is wrong? It is really difficult to understand why these dumb fish would discriminate between the two identical situations. I could believe this if you had caught just one fish, but this defies the laws of probability."

Poor Mike. He was really befuddled. I couldn't resist the opportunity. "Mike, the only thing I can say is that these fish are a lot more discriminating than you think. It must be all the beer, pepperoni, and garlic you ate last night. I'll just bet they are sensitive to the vapor trail you are leaving behind you on your side of the boat! I don't mind telling you that if I was behind you, I would certainly avoid you. Hey—Wow! Feel this baby go! Look at him take line!"

Mike just sat there puzzled. "That is really cute, Ed. I refuse to try another plug. Maybe I'll just reel in and sharpen that hook again."

As Mike began to reel in, I had to ask. "By the way, Mike, how many times have you sharpened the hooks on that plug today? What's the point of sharpening the hooks if they aren't biting at them? I remember reading something in one of the *Angler's Almanacs* that said fish can pick up the smell of humans from hooks if they are handled too much."

Mike looked up with a perplexed look. "You're right, I've sharpened the hooks three times in frustration—but that's hogwash, Ed."

"By the way, the solution is even better, Mike. The book said that if you spit on the plug, the saliva will not only get rid of your smell, it will attract the fish. . . ."

"You know, I've never heard anything so dumb before. I think I will do it just to prove you wrong!"

Well, guess what? Mike was still in the process of pulling out his line when the big one hit!

Tactics. Fish can pick up and discriminate between vibrations through their ears and lateral lines to identify and locate food. Vibrations set up by bait action will attract the fish's attention if it simulates a realistic, locally known vibration.

Concepts and Application. The next highly developed long-range sensory mechanism in the fish is its sound-detection system. The fish hears sound underwater exactly as we hear sounds above water. The big difference is that the fish's hearing ability is amplified by the fact that sound travels about five times faster in water than it does in air. The fish will hear a splash on the water five times faster than we will if we are the same distance away from the source. Fish are also capable of hearing a wide range of sound frequencies almost in the same range as humans. Fish do not have an ear drum so the sounds are received directly, making reception quite effective for long distances. In addition, the fish can identify different sounds just as we can, acting appropriately according to whether the sound is familiar or foreign. A foreign sound will make the fish head for cover, as will a sound which it recognizes as being associated with an enemy. A familiar sound, however, will attract fish, and, very much as they do with their other sensory devices, fish use the sound to seek out or avoid situations. As the fish goes through life, then, he develops an extensive inventory of sounds that allow him to act, or react, well in advance of seeing the sound source.

The fish has another sensory organ that is able to deal with a different aspect of sound, vibrations. The lateral line is a line of sensory nerve endings on either side of the fish which complements the hearing from the ears. Among other capabilities, the lateral line can very accurately pick up low-frequency vibrations, particularly at a close range of less than thirty-five feet. Through this apparatus, the fish picks up sounds which it can learn to identify and store in memory. Any sudden sounds that are detected as foreign will make him flee. Yet another capability of the lateral line is its directional-detection ability. This can allow the fish to accurately calculate the location of the vibration within thirty-five feet. Typically a fish will use its ears and the lateral line in combination quite effectively to seek out food types—or to avoid danger. This process has evolved as a highly successful survival mechanism which makes the fish capable of detecting and locating many different vibrations, such as those set off during distress actions. This includes the types of rhythms set up by the swimming action of many different creatures, including their own species.

What does this mean to an angler? Think about all those things you drag in the water that are unfamiliar to the fish. The fish will be attracted by a vibration: it will first hear it and then it will pick it up through the corresponding vibrations in its lateral line, and thus target in on the location. This is why the vibrations set up by buzz bombs, spoons, or flatfish are effective. They set up interesting vibrations that attract attention. Once they are attracted by the sound, the fish will locate it by the vibrations. That will get Mr. Fish close enough to see the target and strike at it. Now think about all the other sounds you make above water that are amplified sounds to the fish. You may understand how easy it is to scare fish away. A simple thump on the bottom of the boat will carry amplified sounds through the water that will sound like an explosion to fish.

On the Water. This lake was a new adventure for us. We did not know the lake well and it was really hard to read. Perhaps the combination of weather and lack of relevant tactics were the reasons for poor productivity. The lake was a dark blue-green color, obviously full of algae. It had to be a good lake with ample food in it—perhaps too much food. We had tried just about everything that a sports fisherman could try, with little success. Where were they? How many days did we need to end the drought? "I really don't understand this Mike," I said. "Are we being punished for something we did? The only thing left to try is dynamite. But there have to be fish in this lake. Argh! Maybe we should forget this place."

Mike started to rummage through his box. He was obviously looking for something. "I think that we aren't being smart enough. We have been dragging different flies at different depths, but we need to take better advantage of the fish's abilities. The other factor is that this lake is so dark that these fish must not be able to see more that two or three feet. We need something that will bring these fish to us. Obviously trying to find them isn't working, so let's get them to find us."

I was mystified. Had my brother gone bananas? What did he think we had been doing for two days? Since when did fish come to us? "What do you propose, Mike, dragging a mermaid behind the boat? You got one that looks like a trout hidden in there?"

Mike kept digging in his box, finally emerging with two packages. I was obviously going to get some new secrets out of my older brother.

"Little brother, I have two things here that we need to use. The first one is for you—it's called a buzzer; the second is a three-foot willow leaf. This buzzer I found in this funny little shop in Washington. It is supposed to set up a vibration as you troll it. I have no idea what this vibration is supposed to simulate but it is supposed to set up a rhythm that induces a curiosity in fish, probably like the buzz bomb. These fish use the lateral line like a sonar device so if this sound is even the slightest bit interesting they will come in too see it. Now I have no idea what kind of bug thing this is supposed to be so that's where you enter with your willow leaf. The gold color should show through this water, and the spoons should also set up a vibration—and look like a school of fish. You should drag a yellow plug since that will show best in these blue-green waters. And we should not go too deep, say ten feet?"

Well, what could I say after that? There was no way I could better that story. If it worked, I would never live this one down. On the other hand, perhaps I could learn something. After about ten minutes of dragging our seductive new lures and getting no action, Mike told me to come up closer to surface. Just as I was reeling in slowly, I got that familiar tug. And what a beauty he was. After the third fish, I was beginning to think there was some science behind Mike's story.

Tactics. Fish can identify tastes at two levels, in the mouth and through external sensors on the snout. This provides the fish with a two-stage capability to reject foreign bait before the hook is set. Care should be taken to let the hook set.

Concepts and Application. Fish typically have a dual system of taste to add to their arsenal of survival devices. They have the ability to taste through their mouth and through external sensors. They can tell immediately that something is not the real thing and can even discriminate between various tastes such as bitter, sweet, sour, or salty tastes, just as we can. The sense of taste can be used to determine whether an object such as a lure or plug is recognizable. If a fish has decided to ignore the fact that the object has no smell and take it into its mouth, the lack of taste could still be the trigger that causes it to reject the lure.

There are many cases where the fish seems to swim by and just nudge the bait with its snout. In such cases, the fish are using their external taste sensors, which are located on their lips and snouts. These sensors can be so highly developed that they can be used to "pretaste" the food. So if the smell fails, taste at the first level can be the next test. Either ability can give the fish the chance to reject a foreign object before they decide to bite or take it into their mouths. Wouldn't this be a handy ability to have at a seafood buffet?

At the next level, the fish can taste the bait when it is in its mouth. At this point, the fish can still reject a foreign object. As a matter of fact, the fish can even position the bait in its mouth before it decides to swallow. Needless to say, this sequence of discrimination and rejection can make it difficult to fool a fish long enough to "set the hook." If at any point in this process you try to set it by pulling it, you may yank it away from the fish while he is still trying to figure out what this object is, at the first level of sensing. He may have only nudged it with his nose, so don't be too hasty.

On the Water. The lake was absolutely still. It was now 10:00 A.M. and the fish were rising everywhere. We figured that we would get out at about the same time as yesterday when they had started to rise. Now, suddenly, I could feel the rhythm of the plug cease, followed by a faint nibble. Almost instinctively, I pulled up sharply and started to reel in. There was nothing. Ten pulls out and I sat down in an attempt to regain my composure. "Dammit. That's the third one that's done that to me. I'd better reel in and sharpen the hooks on that plug. This time I am not pulling, I will set the tension looser and let him go." Mike sat quietly, just watching. After reeling in and carefully sharpening the hooks, I set the tension loose so I could pull it out with two fingers easily. After forty pulls and five minutes, I sat back with my feet up pondering those visions of giant trout dragging us across the lake. This time I was not going to be foiled. Wheeeeezzz went Mike's line as it screamed out of the reel. I watched with envy as the fish exploded through the surface. Now it was my turn, I could feel something nibbling. The jerk was almost instinctive, as I jumped up, dropping my beer. But there was no action. Nothing pulled anymore. He was gone.

At this point, Mike looked out from under his stupid-looking hat and began to snort. "I can't stand this any longer. Why don't you just sit down and watch the expert for a while? First you want to yank the hook out of his mouth before he has a chance to put it in his mouth, then, when you finally let him sample it, you yank it out again. Ed, that's pretty funny considering you are always giving me all this technical stuff about the dual sensing and tasting ability of these trout. You've got to let him set the hook."

It wasn't long before Mike's rod tip started to quiver a bit. "Now the idea is too keep cool, Ed, let him take the hook by himself." The quiver stopped. Just as I was about to start laughing and tell the old goof not to be so smart, the rod tip looked like it was going into spasms. The two-pound beauty broke water about eighty feet behind the boat. Mr. Cool let the tension off a bit, stood up slowly, and began a very smug reel in. "You see, kid, you got to let the hook set."

3.6   STAY WITH WHATEVER WORKS

Tactics. When you finally catch a fish, there is always a tendency to try something new or to go to a new area, thus wasting the success. Try to stick with the area, technique, and bait that has just worked and enjoy the fruits of your labor.

Concepts and Application. Your first reaction will be to consider this a bit of a stupid principle. Why, you might respond, would I change to a new area or use a new lure if I have just landed a beauty? The answer is rooted in basic human nature. In more cases than you would care to admit, there will be a natural tendency to think that there is an even better spot to fish, and because you think that there is an even bigger brute down there that may prefer a better lure, you will change tactics. It takes more discipline to stay with the same formula than you think— because you are never satisfied with how successful the formula is! If you do change, you risk wasting part of those two hours of precious time when the fish are feeding actively.

  The tactic is not too difficult to adhere to if you really think about it. If you have spent a fair amount of effort going through a process of elimination to catch a fish, why not continue to use the same process in the same area. You have probably caught a fish because you have found a hot spot and you have selected a hot feeding time. Why waste it by changing lures and waters? Enjoy the prospect while you can. Even if you have fluked a catch, why knock it? Use the same tactic in the same area. Sweep over the same area that was productive. In most cases, you will have found a school of trout. If you want to experiment, have your buddy try something else—in the same waters!

On the Water. The fishing was hot. We were about a half hour into the feeding frenzy. They were big but they were cautious. Worst of all, they were picky. We had spent the previous 2 hours trying numerous things at numerous depths. You could feel the fish sampling the bait before they took it. In the past 15 minutes, both Mike and I could feel them cautiously sampling the silver and blue number 4 flatfishes that we were trolling. For some reason, they just weren't aggressive, but when they hit, wow did they hit. It took me 10 minutes to land the big one. "Man these fish are picky," Mike mumbled. "They are not taking the bait, or the hooks aren't setting. Maybe these hooks are too big—I think I should try a number 3."

Mike was about halfway in when I felt the next one give me the big double jerk. This one was a beauty—2 pounds of silver dynamite! It was now about an hour into the big frenzy, Mike was at 50 pulls and a bit deeper. He figured that he would go deeper for a 5-pounder. It was only 10 minutes after I got my number 3 out when the next one hit. Mike had to put his beer down and do the honors on the netting. This was now my third, and Mike was still sitting there waiting. "Mike, why don't you try the silver and blue number 4?" I suggested. "This isn't going to last much longer."

"Ed, you just got lucky. Just watch what happens when I go down another 5 feet—I can feel it in my bones."

Well, while Mike was still feeling his bones, number 4 fish hit my bait like a ton of bricks. "I think I'll play this one for a while, Mike—you just keep feeling those bones while I land this one without a net." Half an hour later, Mike was still dragging his polka dot number 3, looking for the 5-pounder. But the feeding time was over. The score was Ed 4, Mike 0.

4   WHEN DO I FISH?

The last major question is *when*—when is the best time to increase my odds of catching fish? Unless it is your desire to work the water all day long to find the best time at which fish are feeding, or you just want to be out on the water communicating with nature, you may want to consider trying to select the time of day when fish are most likely to feed. No one will say that there is a science to this, but there are a few tactics that can assist you.

If you think back to the previous chapters, you will see that you have gained some insight into when to fish. This information was offered in the explanations of some of the fish's habits, instincts, and abilities. The section on the changing environment, for example, gave you a glimpse of how the fish must constantly adjust to changing elements. You will now perhaps understand why every book you read will tell you to fish in the early morning and the late evening. But although this may be a great piece of advice, it does in no way guarantee that you will hook a fish at those times. The fact is that there are no guarantees, but fish will *most likely* feed at dawn and dusk, so to increase your chances of success, you would logically go out at that time. If you are really keen, you can go out in the morning and maybe catch your limit, but what do you do the rest of the day? The big problem is that most of us mortals like to fish during the daytime. Getting out at 5:00 A.M. or fishing in the cool dusk has its occasional appeal, but let's not push it! Maybe this explains why we don't catch as many fish? Because we choose *our* preferred time and not the fish's.

Fortunately, just as we anglers like to feed in a cyclic fashion, so do fish. And they feed for limited periods. Not only that, but they also have a tendency to feed in a group action. The trick, however, is to figure out when they will decide to dine. It is not as simple as breakfast at 8:00, lunch at 12:00, and dinner at 6:00. Nevertheless, fish do seem to have their own rhythmic timing which we, in all our scientific genius, do not yet understand. The crucial piece of news to us daylight fishermen is that fish will feed together and they do have active feeding times, not necessarily at dawn or dusk. This is encouraging, but it still leaves us with the problem: when do I fish? In this chapter, we will explore some ideas on how to answer this question.

4.1 FISH DURING ACTIVE FEEDING PERIODS

Tactics. Fish feed according to a rhythm because of metabolic processes of digestion and energy loss. This is usually only once or twice a day, in group action, and lasts for less than three hours. The best fishing times will be during these times.

Concepts and Application. In the previous chapters, there have been many suggestions that the fish feeds in some sort of rhythmic fashion—more or less. We have even looked at some of the physiological elements that reinforce this idea. What we have not really covered are the fish's physiological limitations. First of all, we need to understand that there are metabolic reasons for fish to feed in a cyclic fashion. We all know that they will feed in active sessions for a limited time, then stop. Why? We noted in the previous discussions that fish control their energy output very carefully and are keen to conserve energy. The metabolic reality is that they simply cannot afford to waste energy so if and when they do, they will need to wait quite a while to replenish energy for a new feeding frenzy.

But let us back up a bit. If you have spent any time on the water, you soon come to the realization that what will work one day will not necessarily work the next day. You will also note that even on two seemingly equal days, the time at which you catch fish can be quite different. This is most evident during periods when they rise to surface. The fact is that there are active and inactive times during the day when fish, like other animals, decide to look for food with some degree of aggression. Sometimes they are fierce and sometimes they are not, but they do not seek food all day long any more than we do. Just as we are active seeking food three times a day, fish also seek food. They feed and then rest to digest the food. But fish do not wear wristwatches so it is most likely that other more subtle instinctual timing systems are triggered. Yet another predictable observation is that the feeding period is limited, lasting somewhere between a short twenty minutes to a longer three hours. Guess it depends on whether they are having a fondue or visiting McDonald's!

Well, as you may have deduced by now, there are several reasons for this behavior. They can be grouped into three categories: mainly metabolic, instinctual, and environmental. Let us summarize from earlier chapters.

Metabolic. Two major factors will force a fish to feed actively in some form of cyclic pattern. First, digestion takes several hours (up to twelve hours, typically), being a chemical process which is a function of body temperature (same as water temperature). If the water is cool, it can take much longer. As digestion is occurring there may be little reason for fish to pursue more food simply because he hasn't been activated by the hunger trigger. So if a school of fish prefer to laze around in a thermocline, and all eat together, it is quite likely that they will digest at the same rate and be hungry again at about the same time. Secondly, the fish has only so much energy for active feeding. Twenty minutes to two hours seems to be about the limit. Another cyclic characteristic which forces inactive time is the need to rejuvenate the energy level if any exertion has taken place to expend energy. Active feeding and swimming will inevitably force the fish into a rest period, which can take many hours, even up to a day, particularly if there has been any exhausting chases. Because water has four times the heat capacity of air, it can absorb heat very fast from the fish so he has to keep quiet to rejuvenate himself.

Instinctual. Fish are highly competitive. Because of their effective sensing abilities, they can hear, smell, or even see other fish feeding; this can be realized over lengthy distances. This more often than not will result in a chain reaction which gets more fish feeding because others are doing so. It can start by a fish jumping to create a "splat" on the water. Many times this can result in quite a frenzy. This aspect creates the end effect of group feeding frenzies. Either they feel they will miss some choice goodies or they detect an opportunity, but, regardless, they can begin to feed quickly and actively. Another factor that adds fuel to this group frenzy idea is that fish also have some social tendencies—they do tend to school together for "social reasons." Either they feel better protected, or they feel there are more chances of finding food, or possibly there are reproductive reasons at work. When you consider this social action of schooling, it is not that difficult to understand why they may all start feeding together. Finally, the tendency for them to attach themselves to a site, particularly one that has food and shelter, also helps to reinforce the groupie-feed theory.

Environmental. Another aspect that can affect metabolism directly is the water (and air) temperature, as we discussed earlier. As the external air cools and winds blow, the water temperatures shift, thereby affecting the level of activity among the fish. These factors, and night and day variations, have direct effects on when fish will feed. Tides are another factor that impact on feeding times. The other habits of smaller fish, insects, larvae, or other morsels that they feed on may also behave according to their own rhythms. Their increase in activity can then trigger feeding activities in trout. What is also important is to realize that we are dealing with a species of animal that lives by genetically inherited sophisticated instincts that we do not completely understand. In many situations, these instincts seem to be triggered by something that makes fish feed in a mass, during preferred periods, and in an aggressive fashion.

The conclusion is that regardless of what triggers fish to feed actively, they have a tendency to do it in unison, and in many cases the frenzy has a tendency to last up to two or three hours at most. It goes without saying that these are the preferred fishing times. There is no doubt that these feeding times are the most desirable to find. So if you want to minimize time on the water, and maximize your fun reeling in fighters, seek out these times.

On the Water. It was getting to be a bit boring on the water. After four hours, the serenity was being obscured by the drone of the motor. My beer was finished and Hope had finished reading her book. If it hadn't been for the wildlife and the peaceful tranquillity, I might have been disappointed. After all, we were there to catch those giant rainbows that were lurking in the shadows below us. Mike had changed lures and counted so many pulls that he was beginning to look like a mechanical drone at the end of the boat. It seemed that every time I looked up, Mike was mechanically counting pulls. I could sense a frustration in the air. He was starting to look like it was time to be going in for the day. We had stopped the elimination process and tried just about everything. The girls were beginning to glance at each other, snickering quietly. The two technical wizards of deductive reasoning were beginning to run out of ideas. It was exactly 2:00 o'clock in the afternoon when I heard a big "plop" over to the left. The sun had disappeared behind the clouds, and had been there for about twenty minutes now.

Even through the drone of the motor, the splat could be heard loud and clear as the trout's belly flopped on the water. Suddenly we were all wide awake; we watched the ripples radiating out from the epicenter—he was a whale! Then, just ten seconds later, as we continued to stare at the ripples, a second flash of silver left the water, about 100 feet behind the boat. Mike leaped up as if he had been stung by a hornet. His beer fell over and crashed to the floor. The rod tip went into spasms as the fish realized he was hooked, and then he took off like a bullet. Mike's reel sounded like a siren—wheeeeezzz. "Holy sheeeit—look at him go!" Mike gasped. "I've never seen them strike like that!" Just as Mike began to take up some line, I felt a familiar tug. The rod tip gave a few little jerks, then I felt an incredible pull. "Dammit, I must be snagged, what a rotten time for this to happen—no, its loose again—wow! There he is!" A three-pounder broke surface. What a sight! Now you could see fish rising everywhere. The lake looked like it was being pelted with cannon balls from the sky. Just then, Hope's line started to scream as it tried desperately to get out of the reel.

It was just fantastic, you couldn't get your line out fast enough before another beauty broke the water. Bev was the net lady. If anyone would have had a chance to film this netting activity, they would have laughed for weeks; it was as much of a frenzy as the fish feeding. We fished in a frenzy, too, not even bothering to sharpen hooks and count the pulls. These all became a tedious interference with the excitement.

It was precisely 3:25 when everything stopped. No plops, no nibbles, nothing. They had obviously had enough and it was time to rest. And believe me, we all needed the rest after that session.

If you have ever hit such a time, you remember it for a long, long time. This is the way it is, no warning, no indications, no apparent reason, but fantastic to be in. The fish were triggered into feeding by something which happened, and it lasted for only a short time. Let us now look at some ways of picking these times.

4.2   FISH DURING SOLAR CHANGES

Tactics. The sun controls the night and the day light, having a direct impact on the fish's feeding rhythms. The extreme cases are dawn and dusk, which are typically active feeding times for fish.

Concepts and Application. This is a fancy way of telling you to fish in the early morning or late evening, the times when the sun rises and sets. The section on silhouette fishing gave a good explanation of why this is so. Although fish may bite at any time of day, it is agreed between "experts" that the first two hours after daybreak and the last two hours before dark are likely active surface feeding times for fish. In the foregoing discussions, we have pointed to many reasons for this to be so. Here are seven reasons why a fish should feed at dawn:

1. The fish take twelve hours to digest food
2. They wake up hungry
3. Their day vision is ready to go at daybreak
4. The water is cooler, particularly at surface
5. Surface water can mix with oxygen
6. They are well rested with energy levels high
7. Other creatures, including food, are active

Under such conditions, all you need is someone to start feeding to trigger a feeding frenzy. This is all well and good, but if you are like most anglers, the crack of dawn is a bit of a challenge to meet, so you may want to seek out other times during the day, such as the late evening.

We can only hypothesize that as dark approaches, the feeding habits could be stimulated in preparation for the long fast through the night. Sort of like us eating dinner at sundown. Evening feeding can be equally active, but not quite as predictably active. Here are some reasons why a fish should feed at dusk:

1. The fish adjust their vision to acute night vision
2. The light intensity has decreased
3. The evening has cooled the surface waters
4. Other life such as insect life is active
5. The fish needs "supper" before "bedtime"

We need to go a step further, however. Solar changes cause subtle weather changes. Simple cloud cover is, in fact, a solar change, since it changes the light intensity. It has been pointed out that fish do not like bright light, so if the sun is bright, the fish will go down into darker waters or seek shaded areas. If the sun is covered by clouds, or goes down, the fish will be happy to forage actively in shallower waters. This does not mean, however, that this can create an active feeding time.

On the Water. We had planned to spend four days on this lake. It was a small lake in the high country, one that we had never been to. The first day was the one that we would use to get a feel for the lake, so we had planned to spend the whole day on the lake. The locals had given us many clues about what to use and where to try. "The best is a muddler fly made out of deer hair," one of the local camp experts told us, "but you can draw them out with Spratleys and mosquitos. I've caught some good ones on flatfish, and the odd plug, but they seem to be particular about the color." Said the old gentleman, "Over there, where the stream enters the lake, is a long, deep channel—they seem to hang about in that area most of the time. I've heard tell that six-pound trout are in that hole. Why, my brother just caught a five-pounder last week."

That was all we needed to hear. It was a long time since we had caught anything that big. It was time to launch a more serious attack on these monsters; but this time we thought it was time to break tradition. We were going to try fishing at dawn! We thought that the best time to try this was at the beginning of the trip while we were still keen. This would be a pretty difficult experience for us; the girls would no doubt refuse to even consider getting out of the sack at 4:00 A.M. But if we could catch one six-pound fish, it would be worth it.

The evening was stormy. A thunderstorm moved in from the north and the rain was intense. It was a fantastic evening, listening to the rain pelting the shake roof. We were all out like a light at 10:00 P.M., after our tackle and plans were put in place. The storm continued throughout the night. Morning came fast—3:30 is an awful time for a mortal to rise on a vacation—but we were on the water, heading for that deep channel at 4:00 A.M. It was still quite dark and it was actually hard to believe that we were out here. Fortunately, the storm had stopped just before we left the dock—a good piece of luck. The sky was now clearing and the wind stopped. The lake was losing its chop. And just over the landscape you could see the light glowing faintly over the horizon as dawn started to break. We had actually forgotten how fantastic this could be. At 4:20 we were cruising over the channel, Mike with a tom thumb just below surface and me dragging a blue flatfish. You could see signs of fish rolling and surfacing. Maybe these fish had dropped to the bottom for twelve hours and missed a meal because of the storm. Could we be lucky enough to encounter some ravenous trout?

"Ed, this has to be a perfect scene—it's a classic textbook situation—why haven't we had a strike yet? Pass me the thermos." Just as Mike reached over to take the thermos, his rod end jerked and the rod snapped against the floor. He grabbed for it in sheer panic. Mike had set the tension tight, expecting a whale to bite. Now that the whale was on the line, it was about to pull his rod out of the boat. What a sight! The thermos crashed to the floor just as the fish broke water. It was an incredible thing to see in the low light. Then my rod tip started its dance.

For the next two hours, we had the fishing experience of our lives. Four-pound fighters were everywhere, and they were ready to eat. By sunrise, we had our limits. Now we truly understood what active morning fishing was really like.

Tactics. Just as tide tables can be used to predict active feeding times on the oceans, the same tactics can be applied to fresh water, where they can be used to predict possible good feeding periods. Solunar tables and tide tables define such times, which should be fished to maximize productivity.

Concepts and Application. There are always times when you seem to depend on luck to hit a feeding time. We all know that there are times when the fish feed in a frenzy and other times when they are less fierce; they will ignore feed on one day and strike hard another. And when a frenzy starts, it typically lasts for two hours. Sometimes when the frenzy hits, they will take almost anything you drag in front of them. The fact of the matter is that we have all observed preferred periods of time during the day when fish feed in greater numbers and with greater aggression. Although there does not seem to be much consistency in these periods, there are patterns that can be detected.

A lesson may be taken from the use of tide tables on the ocean. Tide tables are a readily acceptable aid that help identify specific times of the day to fish. Tide tables have been produced as a result of knowing the positions of the moon throughout the year. In simplistic terms, the magnetic pull of the moon will have the end result of "pulling" the water away from the land, known as "ebb," or toward the land, known as "flood," depending on where the moon is and how close it is to the earth. The intensity of this pull will, of course, vary, causing the difference in the high and low tides; the time difference as the moon changes positions will also vary. It should be noted that the variation in water height is not unique to the ocean. The same sort of action occurs on other bodies of water, though not to the same degree because of the smaller volume of water.

To an angler, the tide tables and the times shown represent key periods when certain things happen that can stimulate feeding in fish. Thus, to most anglers, the correlation with tide times is indirect rather than direct. It is worthwhile to look at a few of these because they seem to have a direct relevance to trout fishing.

Slack water. Expert fishermen pay much attention to the two hours surrounding slack water when tides change. When the incoming tide (flood) meets the outgoing (ebb), the two flows come together to create a time of "slack water." This time, which is not normally any longer than a few hours, gives fish a chance to move around without battling currents, and to chase other fish that also may become active. Where the two opposite currents meet, a "tide line" is formed as a line of froth and junk that marks the join of waters. This foam and debris attracts feeding birds and various other life forms to create a gathering place for all marine life. As the tide comes out from the land, it carries debris and foodstuff that will attract this activity, and this will also attract feeding fish. Slack water will occur for about a two-hour period around high tide and around low tide. Both of these times should be considered as possibilities for heightened fishing activities. In the next section, we will discuss these as minor (high tide) and major (low tide) feeding periods.

Water flow. Also mentioned in the *where* chapter were the eddies and pools that were created as a result of water movements. The tide tables, and the difference in height, can give you an indication of the degree of current and its direction. If the water flows past a point of land, in a southerly direction, then back eddies will form on the downside. If a specific fishing hole is known to be good, then you can predict the best time of circulating water that will interest the fish (bringing in food) and at the same time offer areas of protection from harsh currents. The water flow, regardless of intensity, will have a tendency to disturb and move small organisms, particularly algae. Such action will activate the food chain participants to feed.

Flood tide. Quite often, feeding occurs when an area becomes flooded by a high tide, allowing fish to come into areas not readily accessible at other times. This creates feeding opportunities that can trigger things, and is quite easily predicted as the high tide time.

The above all serve in helping the fish "decide" when to start setting out the cutlery. The tide tables just allow you to predict ahead of time when this could be. It is important to point out that the same tidal effect takes place on lakes; it is simply reduced substantially so that it is not noticeable. The fact is that the moon pulls lake waters just as easily as it does the ocean waters. The effects are much more subtle, but, nevertheless, they are still there. The overall effect of this is not noticeable on a small lake because the body of water is not large enough to be affected by a direct gravitational pull. It is much more pronounced on large lakes where you will actually get a rise and fall of the lake level. Nevertheless, it is worth repeating, regardless of size, the tidal pull is still there.

The other consideration in all this is that we seldom fish the same waters consistently enough to determine any patterns, so we have a tendency to disbelieve any correlation with lunar mechanisms, but there is no doubt that the sun and the moon play key roles in influencing feeding habits. Most experts will verify that the sun and moon are causing situations that get the fish active. This is the "causal" approach, suggesting that the moon causes it indirectly; it does not "trigger" the fish to act directly. Such a suggestion could prove to be a bit off base, weird, even goofy. But whether we believe it or not, these two celestial bodies may influence behavior more than we like to admit. And just because our scientists can't provide definitive proof that the moon triggers certain activities, this does not mean that it isn't so. After all, do we know all the laws of behavior? Hardly. For a few moments, let's go a step further. Let us not forget the human desire to eat three meals a day according to the cycles of the sun. Let's not forget the fact that we sleep when the sun sinks and wake when it rises. Is this because it gets dark?

A *solunar period* is a word coined to reflect solar and lunar odd-hour periods when heightened activities can be predicted in various wildlife. The lunar day has twenty-four hours, within which four odd-hour periods occur. Solunar combines the solar and lunar cycles. The suggestion is that the sunup and sundown cycles have a dramatic effect on fish feeding, and may even predict the intensity. Consider the moonup and moondown as another possibility. Just because you can't see it, doesn't mean it isn't happening; the moon has its own up and down just like the sun, as well as its own intensity. This is most obvious when the full moon rises over the horizon. Remember that fish are quite capable of seeing in the moonlight, so to a fish, moon up could be just as good as sun up. Well, these cycles are quite predictable, and the various up and down cycles of the sun and moon are detailed in a set of tables, called solunar tables, that can be purchased, much like tide tables.

Solunar tables are produced by Mrs. Richard Alden Knight out of Montoursville, Pennsylvania, on a yearly basis. These tables provide a major and minor period (usually each day) that gives you the period of activity. Major periods last around two hours while minors are forty-five to ninety minutes. The times are corrected according to location away from standard meridians and time zones so that you are able to do a simple calculation to determine when the major or minor time would occur on the body of water that you are fishing. The great thing about this is that you can use this on lakes, anywhere, the same as tide tables are used on the ocean.

In reality, solunar tables simply give you a time which has a direct correlation with tide tables. The solunar "minor period" is the slack tide time around a high tide, while the solunar "major period" is the slack tide surrounding the low tide. The solunar periods suggest these minors and majors are the best times to get your line out, and they last from twenty minutes to over two hours. There's nothing new about this when we think about the material discussed in the earlier chapters; and there's nothing new about this to a salmon fisherman on the ocean. Most sport shops have a copy of the solunar tables; just ask for them.

We find that many fishing lodges secretly have a copy of the solunar tables under the counter, or placed in an inconspicuous place with maps, brochures, and local information. We find that most experts resist mentioning the idea for fear they may be branded a heretic and that this would destroy their credibility. Well, why should the privilege of using celestial bodies be reserved for salmon fishermen? If you use tide tables on the ocean, try the same concept on fresh water lakes. You may surprise yourself and hit a feeding frenzy. The idea that fish (and animals in general) become increasingly active, and are most likely to feed, on the basis of the phases of the moon is hardly a new idea, yet to some people who regiment their activities according to the sun and moon, this is quite absurd. Yet an analogy is useful: there is no law of science that will prove that humans eat breakfast just after the sun rises because, statistically, one can show that everybody does not eat "brekky" when he wakes in the morning, and that some even don't wake. Nevertheless, the *majority* reflect a behavioral pattern that can be used to predict a most likely activity time. So if I wanted to select a time when most humans in a certain area were going to be eating, then knowing the movement of the solar body might be a pretty good predictive tool.

It must be noted that these "hot times" can be disturbed by changes in weather, barometric levels, and temperature, so the idea is that this is not an absolute method; it only identifies the most likely time when fish will feed. If you want to increase your chances of hitting a feeding time, then this is the way to do it. The primary thesis is that birds and animals, and perhaps even humans, become more active during these periods. Most experts and scientists give little scientific credibility to this statement; however, we feel through experience that it really enhances your chances: when fish feed in a frenzy, it is most often a solunar period. So you can take this for what it is and test it for yourself. But when you hit a really good fishing period, just ponder the mysteries of life for a moment and consider that maybe the moon may be triggering the activity directly. And maybe the difference between low and high tide has a direct correlation with the feeding intensity? Think about that one.

On the Water. The evening was upon us and we had settled into the cabin; time to recall the fishing highlights of the day. Unfortunately, there were few fish to show for our efforts, except for some small ones. But the highlight was when Mike decided to cast a new plug from the boat and caught his pants, and his skin. It was a rather fierce cast, so he managed to get the treble hook well set in his behind. It probably didn't feel too great to Mike, but it sure was funny.

We had planned to fish during a major period, which we calculated as starting at 2:00 P.M. Mike had forgotten his solunar tables so I had to pull the Vancouver tide tables out of the truck. The tide tables indicated that, in Vancouver, the low tide was at 12:30 P.M. Adding an hour for daylight saving time made this 1:30 P.M. Looking at the map, we were about 250 miles inland from the coast so we added thirty minutes as about the time that a low tide equivalent would be at the lake. As a rough guide, we figured to add about thirty minutes for every 250 miles eastward. To adjust for errors due to Mike's astronomical "expertise," we decided that we would need to get out well before this time and fish through the "hot period." But the weather had been unsettled and stormy, dumping rain sporadically. In fact, we were out there by 11:00 A.M. The wind had picked up to stir up the water, continuing to create a steady chop that made trolling difficult. We fished the hot period faithfully, but with little success. The storm had probably sent them deeper. The fishing was dismal, except for the odd small one that we had to throw back. The only salvation was that no one else had much of a good day either. This we found out when we came in, in the late afternoon.

But it was time to plan out the next day's strategy, and Mike had one. "Tomorrow the major hot time would be at about 2:30 P.M. Ed, I have a better feeling for us limiting out. The weather is supposed to settle down as well. We should fish a few hours in the morning but let's go out with our whole arsenal at 1:30 P.M. The area where the creek cuts a channel into the lake will be hot for sure. That's where we got the nibbles today."

The next morning was indeed glorious. It was a treat to meet it. Our morning fish was mediocre, hauling in just enough for our late breakfast. But the afternoon session was very different. We knew the most likely feeding depth, and the most likely bait, so we had a head start. We got out there at 1:30 P.M. but there was no action. It was about 2:20 when things started to happen, just out of nowhere. We had actually settled back to enjoy the scenery and the tranquillity of it all when it started. It was incredible. It takes a special place in our lexicon of fish stories to this day.

The point of this is that if there is anything that you can use to select a time, then it should be used. There are hot times, just as there are hot spots. There is no guarantee that they will be so but why not accept a certain degree of error and try to increase your odds of selecting the time?

5   TECHNICAL ANALYSIS

This is finally where you make a science of it. This chapter is for the "techies." Here we present two simple components of technical analysis that are founded on the previous material. The purpose is to answer the where, what, when questions quickly. The idea builds on the process of elimination that can be applied quite readily to any lake or body of water even before you set your boat out on the water. Call it "armchair angling" if you like; all you need is to remember some of the key conclusions of the previous chapters. The next step that the techie would take would be in the field, or on the water. Here you would check out the armchair analysis by keeping a record of your activities. Let's back up a bit first.

Technical analysis is a way of quantifying the basic ideas brought out in the previous chapters—on paper. In reality, the process of elimination is being shifted from the field to the office. All you are doing is trying to read a picture of a body of water and its surrounding terrain to decide on smaller and smaller areas that give you the better opportunities to find the fish. Since the fish will rarely come to you, you need to find them. Since fish do not move too far from sources of food and shelter, it would make sense to select the areas that appear to satisfy these conditions.

The basis for this investigation requires a *lake survey map* which shows the depth of the water, and a *land survey map* to show the lay of the land, in terms of terrain elevation along with numerous other features such as roads, creeks, rivers, and so on. This investigation can be carried out at home. This can then be refined while on the lake.

The final part of the technological process is carried out while fishing, by keeping records of your fishing efforts over the duration of the trip, in the form of a simple log. The fishing log is a simple but effective way of refining the technical process.

5.1 APPLY A TECHNICAL ANALYSIS

Tactics. Any body of water can be subjected to a technical analysis using topographic maps and lake survey maps. The areas of most likely fishing productivity can be identified using a systematic analysis procedure that isolates temperature, shelter, and food areas most likely to harbor fish.

Concepts and Application. To explain this simple process, we need to consider an example lake. For this, we will use Rainbow Lake, which we are going to fish in summer. Rainbow Lake is several miles long, nestled in the mountains of the interior of British Columbia. It is not completely remote from civilization, but an effort is required to drive to it through the mountains. It is a cold-water lake at 3,000 feet in elevation, freezing over in the winter, but thawing rapidly in the spring. The lake has a lodge and cabins where you can rent a boat to catch the fighting rainbow trout. Reports are that four- to five-pound fish are common but that they are moody feeders. Since we have never been here, we are going to perform a technical analysis of this lake before we venture northward.

In looking back at what we discussed in the previous chapters, there were some simple things about the fish's behavior as related to metabolism, food, and shelter that we need to recall.

Metabolism. The fish needs to find a thermocline where he can get oxygen and proper temperature. This layer is most likely to be somewhere between twenty and forty feet below surface in the summer, deeper as summer progresses.

Shelter. Certain physical structures and features were preferred because they could offer the fish protection from predators or refuge from harsh elements. These could be quiet waters on shelves, drop-offs, near cliffs, close to places to hide, or in the shade areas of the lake.

Food. Any waters that would contain feed fish, desirable food, or other feed areas were of particular interest to a fish. These could be overhanging brushes where insects drop off, vegetated areas where various food (frogs, leaches, worms, etc.) could be found, streams which empty into the water, bays where other food sources could exist.

Let us consider how this information would be used on Rainbow Lake. It would be reasonable to conclude that if you looked at the whole lake, your best bet in finding fish would be to fish in the layer of water that is twenty to forty feet deep. But trying to cover the whole lake might be silly because another good bet is that fish are hanging about in sheltered areas away from open water, unless that open water is in contact with the thermocline and has some bottom protection. The next consideration is that they spend a majority of time resting and hiding. So it would make sense to locate any areas on the lake that are obvious natural structures that offer the fish protection. If we can find areas where shelter can be found in a thermocline, then this would be an even better bet to find fish. Thus, any place that the thermocline was against a rock wall with a ledge would represent a good area to target. If there is shade in the area, it would be better. Well, this simple set of deductions forms the basis for a simple analytical process that can be quantified on a lake survey map.

Carrying this concept to the next step, if we could find the areas where good food sources were combined with the thermocline and good shelter, we would have an even better target area to fish. Thus, if a stream empties into the area, or deep weeds harbor feed fish, or overhanging vegetation drops insects, these would all provide food sources for fish.

What you are doing here is a very simple process of elimination on the basis of selecting those waters which contain the best combination of elements that the fish require to satisfy their physiology and instincts.

The big question is how would this be analyzed on paper? To do this, you need a map such as the one shown here of Rainbow Lake. This type of map is produced by the Canadian Hydrographic Services (for oceans) in the form of nautical charts, or by the Fisheries Department that produce hydrographic charts of inland lakes. They cost a mere $3.50 or so and there is a fairly extensive list of lakes that have been surveyed this way. Equivalent charts are available in the U.S.A.

Figure 12 is a typical lake survey map. It shows Rainbow Lake. It identifies the lake edge, depth of water, and an island in the middle. It is quite obvious from the contours that the water deepens rapidly on the northern shoreline, then shallows toward

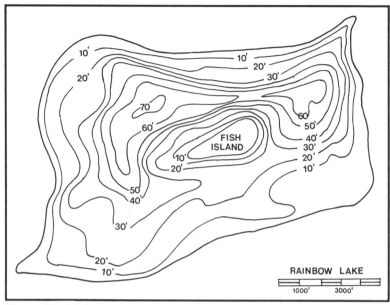

Figure 12. A lake survey map of Rainbow Lake

the island and most of the south shore. It is quite obvious that the water flow through the lake is probably through the northern channel, which deepens to seventy feet in places. The whole southern shore is most often less that thirty feet deep. If you had never seen the lake, let alone fished it, you would already know more of its secrets than most fishermen who fished it. You can see a deep hole at the two ends of the lake, which go to over sixty feet. This is really not a deep lake, but a perfect habitat for trout if there is food in the lake.

Because you are planning to fish in the early summer, it would be reasonable for you to seek out the best temperature zone. Knowing about thermoclines, and the fish's need to find compatible temperature and oxygen, you could conclude that the most likely place in the lake would be in a thermocline layer between twenty and forty feet.

So you would take your lake survey map and fill in the area between the twenty- and forty-foot contour lines. This would be *step one* of your technical analysis. We have used right-sloping diagonal lines to show this. This would look like the map in

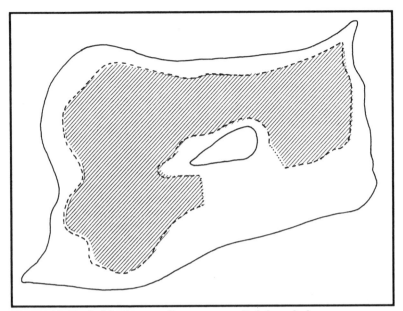

Figure 13. Probable thermocline areas on Rainbow Lake

Figure 13. The filled in area is a simple analysis of the first step in the elimination process that was discussed in Chapter One. All you have done is to decide where on the lake you should (and should not) troll on the basis of water temperature.

Note that you have quickly eliminated a vast portion of the lake simply because it would be too shallow and the water would be too warm: the whole southern shoreline is less than twenty feet deep. If you didn't know the depth, then you would be out on the lake and probably losing a few lures before you figured this out the hard way.

So the map now shows the waters that would contain the full thermocline, which we believe to be between twenty to forty feet deep. The next step would bring in the concept of *protection*. The fish would naturally prefer areas along shore rather than open water. This area would be a smaller area within the thermocline, but close to shore. This is not to say that the fish will not frequent the other areas of the thermocline; it only suggests that the preferred trout area will be away from open water, unless the thermocline is in contact with the bottom. Such a case may exist

101

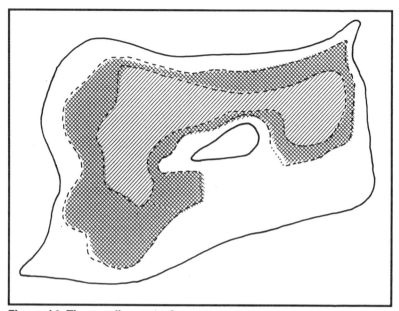

Figure 14. Thermocline away from open water

along the southern shore, where it gets to thirty feet. In all likelihood, this area, being directly exposed to sun, and featuring slow-moving water, would be too warm in summer. It would be a good bet in spring and fall. At any rate, the area may warrant some bottom-bumping technique.

If we draw another set of diagonal lines going the other way, then we get a picture like Figure 14. The double set of diagonals now shows us the next, "better," area. The double diagonal area would be preferable to the single because it now meets two constraints.

Now, let us read some more information off the lake survey map, continuing on the idea of *shelter and protection.* We know that the fish prefer to stay within protected areas such as ledges, close to points of land, or around drop-offs because these provide them with some means of protection from elements and predators. Furthermore, the preferred areas would be those that are contained within the thermocline that we just highlighted. If we were trying to select these areas within the twenty- to forty-foot area, we would look at areas where the contours become

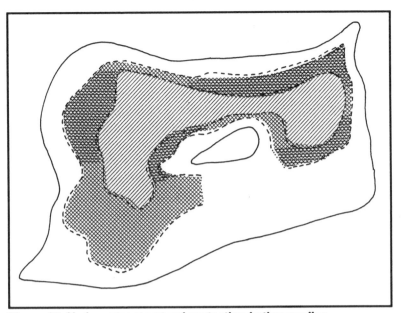

Figure 15. Underwater structural protection in thermocline

wider apart just within the thermocline, or where the depth changes were slow, forming a shelf, then dropping off rapidly.

These areas would offer a shelf to a fish and could be even more desirable. Additionally, where the twenty- to forty-foot contours were close to other structures, such as points of land or coves, or where they were close to shore would provide other good areas. For example, the thermocline coming close to shoreline would suggest that the lake deepens quickly in that area, providing a place where the fish could keep in the shade or keep close to rocks.

So let us draw horizontal lines within these areas to represent our third criteria. This next step would involve marking these areas on the map, staying within the thermocline boundaries. The resulting map would look like the one shown in Figure 15. Where there are three lines, three constraints are satisfied, and these areas would be even more desirable to fish in than the previous two.

You have now read about as much as you can from this map, by attempting to pick out water depths and underwater structures that could interest the fish. The first constraint was *temperature,* the next was *protected water,* and the third was *structural features* below the surface. You have, in a few simple steps, eliminated all but some strips of water that represent these best possibilities for trolling. The areas shown on your analysis map will now reflect the degree of trolling desirability by the density of lines drawn on the map. You would certainly want to start trolling between twenty- to forty-feet deep along the north shore and around the east end—without even seeing the lake!

You have now used most of the information given on the lake survey map. Let us carry the process another step, using a land survey or topographic survey map. This would involve reading a different type of contour map, one depicting the land surrounding the lake, along with other key features. These maps are also

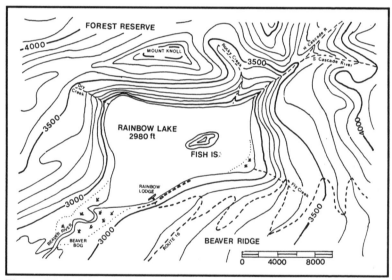

Figure 16. Rainbow Lake area land survey map

available from the U.S. and Canadian Geological Survey Departments and typically provide a great deal of information about the area. Figure 16 shows the topography around Rainbow Lake.

By reading this map, you can continue the last step of your analysis to see protective structural features such as rock bluffs that may not have been obvious from the lake survey map. You

104

can see that the hill rises steeply to the north, into the forest reserve toward Mount Knoll. The terrain steepens quickly to the northeast where the Cascade River enters the northeast end. Beaver River, on the other hand, meanders in a flat area through Beaver Bog. The map offers much information about the area, showing roads, swamps, river, creeks, and so on.

Now, let us continue the analysis by reading more relevant features off this map. This will involve looking at more of the structural features and then looking at the aspect of *food*.

By considering other structural features shown on this map, you would end up adding some additional horizontal lines—still indicating the *third level* of analysis criteria. This would include additional areas like the area north of Fish Island where the drop-off would be in the shade. The steep mountainsides along the north would also offer a protective habitat. In the case of Rainbow Lake, most of the areas have already been analyzed from the lake survey map, so there is little to add; but the resulting target map would identify the best areas of the thermocline to try first.

The *last step* of the armchair analysis would bring in the fourth constraint of *food*. This would include marking those areas which are likely to contain or provide sources of food, such as streams entering, protective coves, vegetated areas, or whatever natural features that are capable of providing food in some way. Some of these may be hard to spot without being on the lake, but certain features are usually quite obvious. At Rainbow Lake, the area to the northeast shows the Cascade River coming down some steep contours to pour into the lake. Obviously this river has carved the deep fishing hole in the northeast corner between the mouth and Fish Island. It has created a deeper channel along the northern shoreline, through the northwest hole and, finally, out to the slow-moving Beaver River. This river would obviously provide a source of food and oxygen well within the thermocline. This area we will mark with vertical lines on the map. The river forms a deep channel into the lake bottom. The river would provide a viable food source. The channel would be deep enough to be in the thermocline and the river flow would provide oxygen mixing. This would be a *likely* hot area for fishing deeper—for those giants.

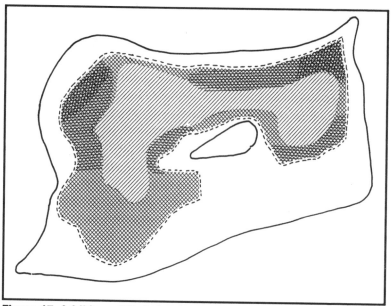

Figure 17. Addition of likely food sources

Another spot is where Rocky Creek comes straight down the mountainside into the lake. There could be a good source for food out from the shoreline. A final area to consider could be where Dry Creek flows out into the shelf below surface, into the deep area of the lake.

The resulting map, Figure 17, now shows the degree of interest to fish. You have methodically read a couple of maps to select where you should, and should not, troll to increase your chances. Before you even get there, you have a vivid analysis of the lake, knowing many secrets that would probably amaze the locals.

Once you have completed your analysis, you will have illustrated, in successive density, the areas that are "hottest" in that they represent the most probable waters that harbor fish most of the time. These represent the areas that you would troll. But the story does not end here. Once you had arrived at the lake, and had a close look at the real features (and opinions), you would mark your fifth level of desirability. You may have even added to number four after a closer inspection of the surrounding terrain. As you spent your days out on the lake, you would undoubtedly add to your analysis.

On the Water. It was early spring in Vancouver and Mike and I were planning an early summer fishing trip. Our choice was a small lake in the interior of B.C. The lake was reasonably close to a small town, just ten short miles up in the hills. This was a narrow lake that we had been to before. The owners were the finest people around and we always had a relaxing time. The great attraction was the fact that the lake was well protected and the boats were spacious. But best of all was the thought of the fighting fish, common to the higher, colder waters. And the cabins were superb, with an uncanny and satisfying combination of rustic and modern conveniences. The place always had its charm, perhaps too much of it since we didn't spend too much time on the lake fishing. This trip was going to be a bit different—we were going to get those big twenty-inch fish that we knew inhabited the lake. This time we were going to make an effort to be very scientific about fishing, so we could select specific areas and times to fish, thereby giving us a good opportunity to enjoy some other activities with the girls and still have a productive fishing excursion. Although we had been there before, we did not really know the lake. We only had simple pictures of the lake layout. So the plan was to perform a complete technical analysis on the lake.

Our strategy was to split up the technical analysis. I would perform the armchair analysis and Mike would complete the analysis by doing the field work upon his arrival. He and Bev had planned to go up a few days before us so the objective of the technical log was his responsibility.

I had ordered the lake survey map and the land survey map and had performed the technical analysis. The final analysis looked like the map in Figure 18. I had found it easiest to combine the two maps into my own drawing. The lake, surprisingly shallow, was long and thin, well protected in the mountains, with cabins overlooking the lake. I had drawn in the areas that covered the thermocline, protected waters, and sheltered areas. Where two and three constraints were satisfied, I marked these as OK and Good. The good spots looked like they would be along the western shore along the northern end of the lake, and the eastern shore just across the lake. Both of these had a shelf into the thermocline. The west side would probably be best in the evening shade, while the east strip would probably be better in

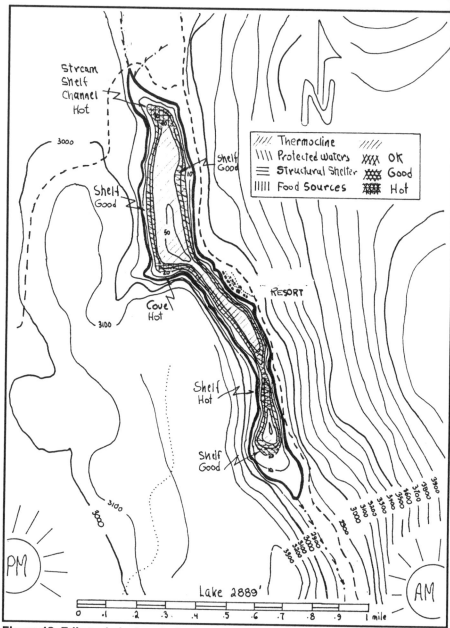

Figure 18. Ed's technical analysis map

the morning. This I noted from the position of A.M. and PM. sun. The area at the south end also looked good, on the basis that a shelf was formed, coming out of a deeper hole just north of it.

By adding information from the land survey map, it was obvious that the stream at the north end of the lake had cut a deeper channel into the thermocline, offering fish an excellent place for food, and containing a shelf as well. This was a good prospect for "hot fishing." Two other areas looked hot, one being in a protected cove nestled along the western shoreline at about mid lake, and another area close to the south end in a saddle that created a shelf in the thermocline. These last two areas would need to be inspected and tested on the field expedition before a final reading could be made. This would be Mike's job.

The map now showed six small areas that represented the best fishing alternatives. "Mike," I said, "you can't possibly miss with all of this superior analysis. The next step is the technical log. That is for you and Bev to produce."

Tactics. Documentation of where, when, and what as you go through your process of elimination helps in the trial-and-error process. The log will help you to remember prior trip tactics or current trip activities to maximize productivity.

Concepts and Application. This, the second component of "technical fishing," is important, but it is yet another simple tactic that is so often overlooked. It is a sure thing that at some time in your angling career you have seen these elaborate tables and books that are called "fishing logs." Many of these logs may be overkill in that they require more information than you have time to fill in. The whole idea behind a log, or log equivalent, is to record your elimination process so that you are simply recording the where, when, what details. It does not take a genius to realize that this simple process either records how you have caught fish, or how you have not caught fish—both useful things to record to help you determine the right spot, time of day, and the bait next time. Furthermore, you will appear as a genius if your current records, or even your previous records from previous trips, get you to the right spot quickly.

This does not mean that you need to write out a technical abstract every time you change a parameter, nor does it mean that you should fill out long tabulations of statistics. All you really want to know are some simple things on what you tried, where you tried it, when, how deep, the number of pulls, and what you caught. Keep it simple.

I have always resisted the idea of keeping a log, simply because I didn't feel it necessary. But I have always wondered why so many experts always write little notes in a tattered and torn booklet. Yet, whenever I have gone to the same place more than once, I have cursed because I cannot remember what worked before, so I go through the same searching process. The log helps avoid this.

On the Water. After a five-hour drive, Hope and I finally arrived at the resort. It was midday and we were anxious to get rid of the city thoughts. It wasn't hard to do this as we looked at the layout, with the cabins nestled in the pines overlooking the tranquil lake.

The air was fresh and warm—typical of the high country in mid-June. The lake looked as inviting as ever, with that dark green emerald look that made you feel that the big ones had grown bigger since last year. Mike and Bev were out to greet us with their usual warm smiles and laughter. Bev had been measuring three big rainbows out on the table. Having been there for two days, they were excited and anxious to share the fishing highlights. "Ed, you wouldn't believe it! We have caught our limits in the last few days," Bev squealed. "It's fantastic!"

Mike handed me a cold beer. He had dog-eared the technical analysis map, which was sticking out of his pocket. Bev handed me this scruffy looking notebook with some cryptic notes under each day. There was no way we were going to get a chance to settle into this place.

"Ed, this is the technical log," Bev reported. "On Sunday we went out and we fished for two hours. I started with a blue and gold flatfish at fifty pulls and a half-ounce weight in the morning. Mike tried his flies but they were not too interested. But last night was the capper—I got my limit!"

The translation of Bev's technical log follows, typed more or less as it was written.

JUNE 15, Gorgeous day with all the birdies out talking to us. Mike a bit growly but he settled down once we were on the water. The lake was still with a slight breeze coming down from the north end.

8:50 AM Nibble on a #3 blue and gold flatfish	*South end*	*half oz. 50 pulls*	*lost him*
9:02 AM Nibble on a #3 blue flatfish	*South hole*	*half oz. 60 pulls*	*lost him*
9:15 AM Bite on a #3 blue and gold	*South hole*	*one oz. 60 pulls*	*10 inches!*
9:30 AM Bite on a #3 blue flatfish	*South saddle*	*half oz. 55 pulls*	*let it go*
10:00 AM Nibble on Doc Spratley	*South saddle*	*third oz. 55 pulls*	*lost it–small*

10:30 AM Heading back to cabin, Mike too grouchy, minor action and wind picking up.

No action on frogs, red plugs and other flies. Silver seems to be the interesting color. No action at depth at all.

2:00 PM, Great day, nice and warm, time to "hustle the buns" because the solunar tables point to a peak period. Mike is all excited, with a "feeling in his bones." Clear sunny day, no wind, got my book and we are off again.

2:10 PM Bite on a Muddler fly	*North cove*	*surface troll*	*9 inches*	*Mike*
2:30 PM Bite on red flatfish #3	*NE shore*	*half oz. 55 pulls*	*12 inches*	*Mine*
2:40 PM Bite on silver/blue flatfish	*NE shore*	*half oz. 55 pulls*	*14 inches*	*Mine*
3:00 PM Bite on blue flatfish	*North end*	*half oz. 60 pulls*	*spit hook out*	*Me*

3:30 PM Nibble on green plug   South shore   one oz. 50 pulls   let go–small   *Mike*

3:30 PM Heading back for pit stop, wind picking up and a small chop starting. Will try a deep troll up the channel. No action on Spratleys, frogs, gold flatfish and red flatfish. No action mid lake or along the south shore. Mike tried a deep troll with 2 oz. with no action. No action on deeper trolling

7:00 PM Time for some evening trolling. The wind is gone and the lake is still. You can see risers from the balcony and Mike is eager. He says he is going to start at surface since they are rising. The plan is to cruise the north shore and head for the end where the stream enters the lake. I've got my book and my snickers bars so I am ready. I think I'll just troll a silver/blue flatfish.

7:10 PM Strike on silver/blue flatfish   North end   half oz. 55 pulls   16 inches WOW! *Mine*

7:15 PM Nibble on a leech(fly)   North shore surface 50 pulls   Mike lost it–tiny

7:20 PM Strike! on silver/blue #3   North end   half oz. 55 pulls   15 inches WOW! *Mine*

7:30 PM Mike agitated, changing to #3 blue and going deeper. He can't take the competition!

7:33 PM Strike on blue flatfish   North end   half oz. 55 pulls   14 inches   *Mike*

7:40 PM No time to write, too much action on blue flatfish, half oz. and 55 pulls is the secret.

8:30 PM Time for a breather, we got 4 beauties in the last 20 minutes.

No action on flies and frogs. Tried 1 to 2 oz. but no action at depth. Best action in the evening on blue flatfish. Best area over the channel at north end and along the northwest shore.

Well, it certainly didn't take a genius to figure out where we would try our luck. The blues were the obvious winners, light weight and fifty to fifty-five pulls. The northwest shoreline and the hot spot at the north end were the obvious winners. We looked at the technical analysis. Mike had made notes by my hot spots. "The cove," he began, "is protected and there is good vegetation. I think that it could really be a hot spot in the evening. We haven't had a chance to check out the northeast shore yet since we got all the action at the north end. There are marshes at the north end bordering the thermocline and that is the hot area so far. I'll bet it is really hot for fly fishing in the late evening."

Need I tell more? It was indeed a good trip.

SUMMARY

It is now time to summarize the vast amount of information that has been presented to you. Secrets are always simple—once you know them. But getting there is usually not so simple. For this reason, we have provided much of the information that "helps you get there," and at times it may have seemed a bit tedious. Nevertheless, we hope that the information has been useful and informative.

Through the chapters, we presented a total of twenty-six tactical secrets. At the risk of being repetitive, let us summarize the secrets and tactics.

Chapter 1 Some Fundamentals

We dealt with some fundamentals, providing six simple tactics that can help you dramatically increase your chances of seeking out and keeping that fish once you have caught one. Let us recap those six simple secrets:

1.1 Use a Process of Elimination

Always try to eliminate the wrong steps and items as quickly as possible. The successful actions will lead you to the best formula but you must try different procedures, depths, and lures to do this effectively—experiment with logical methodology.

1.2 Understand Your Quarry

Knowing a little about the trout's habits, needs, and capabilities will always place you at an advantage. It is useful to know these.

1.3 Monitor Line Distance

The most important means of finding, and remembering, the right depth is through simple pull-and-release techniques. This method should become an automatic mechanism.

1.4 Read Your Rod Tip

Your rod tip is sensitive to underwater actions and reactions.

Learning to read the tip will allow you to also understand what is happening below surface.

1.5 Keep Your Hooks Sharp

The most common cause of losing fish is a dull hook. The simple act of sharpening hooks, or replacing them often, increases your chances of keeping fish substantially.

1.6 Adjust Line Tension

Poorly controlled line tension is the second most frequent cause of losing fish. You must learn to check it often and never keep it too loose or too tight.

Chapter 2 Where Do I Fish?

We dealt with the question of deciding where and where not to fish. We offered another nine simple tactical secrets that you could add to your arsenal. Let us recap:

2.1 Water Temperature is Crucial

Fish are very sensitive to water temperature since it controls their metabolism and their feeding activity. Knowing this, you need to try to find the waters which will be most suitable to the fish.

2.2 Fish in the Summer Thermocline

In summer, lake waters tend to form three layers of water with different temperature ranges. The central one, usually forming at twenty to fifty feet below surface, is the most suitable for trout to forage and survive in.

2.3 Fish Near Surface in Fall and Spring

In the spring and fall, the surface waters tend to cool, allowing fish to become more active close to surface. This is the time to use fishing techniques and bait that are more surface oriented.

2.4 Find Structural Sheltered Areas

Fish will naturally tend to choose sheltered areas which allow them to hide or avoid harsh elements such as currents. They are most likely found in such areas which can be identified.

2.5 Fish Near Natural Food Sources

The next preference will be the food sources. Many likely food sources can be identified and these form areas of water that will naturally attract the fish.

2.6 Use Three Key Trolling Methods

Of all the different trolling methods available, three simple techniques–surface, midwater, and bottom-bumping–will cover just about every level of a lake. These are simple and useful.

2.7 Apply a Depth Iteration Process

Varying your fishing depths is the most effective tactic in finding the fish. It should be done in a methodical trial-and-error fashion until the fish are found.

2.8 Check Out the Lake Water Type

Certain lakes that have clear water are not able to support the organic life that allows fish to thrive. Such lakes are usually identifiable and are a waste of time to fish.

2.9 Ask Some Local Questions

The most effective way of finding out where the fish are and what works best is to simply ask others. This information is usually valuable and offered freely.

Chapter 3 What Do I Fish With?

We discussed the question of what to use. Although we cannot identify the specific baits to use, we are able to offer six secrets that will help you choose the best alternative. Much of this is related to the fish's physiological makeup. Let us recap:

3.1 Use Silhouette Fishing in Low Light

Fish are able to see very clearly in low light—even in moonlight, seeking out food by contrasting recognizable silhouettes against a lighter background such as the sky. Recognizable bait detail, shape, and size are important, not color.

3.2 Vary Lure Color by Lighting

Fish are able to see color, but the surrounding water and lighting controls what colors are actually visible. As depth and darkness increase, the brighter colors like red, orange, and yellow disappear and become gray tones—so they are effective near the surface or in bright daylight. Otherwise, the greens and blues will show best at depth and in low light.

3.3 Avoid Foreign Smells

Fish have highly developed smell capabilities which can alert them of danger or attract them if familiar. This capability should never be underestimated but used to your advantage.

3.4 Simulate Live Bait with Lure Vibrations

Fish sense danger or familiar sources of food on the basis of the vibration. This can be used to attract the fish from a distance.

3.5 Let the Fish Set the Hook

There is always a tendency to yank the hook when a nibble is sensed. This may not be a wise move when the fish is simply trying to decide whether the bait is appropriate. Letting the fish set the hook may be more prudent.

3.6 Stay with Whatever Works

Human nature will naturally tend toward trying something "better" to get something "bigger," even if success is at hand. Because fish feed in rhythms for limited times, it may be better to stick with what has already worked and take advantage of the short feeding time.

Chapter 4 When Do I Fish?

We dealt with the element of timing, offering three more tactical secrets to assist you. Although these are never definite formulas, they help increase your chances of success. Let's recap:

4.1 Fish During Active Feeding Periods

Fish have a tendency to feed actively in a cyclic process for fixed periods of time. There are many physiological reasons for this. It is best to try to seek out these times to increase your chances. These times should be included in the fishing period if possible.

4.2 Fish During Solar Changes

Morning and evening are still tried and true times for good fishing.

4.3 Use Solunar or Tide Tables

Tide tables and solunar tables identify potential peak periods during which fish are likely to feed. These can be used to identify specific time periods that should be included in your chosen fishing time.

Chapter 5 Technical Analysis

We summarized many of the tactics into a technical approach for those who are thusly inclined. There were two important tactical secrets that we offered. Let us recap:

5.1 Apply a Technical Analysis

The process of selecting the best water on any lake can be done at home with a set of maps available from the government. The lake water depths allow you to identify areas that have the best temperature, protection, and shelter while land maps allow you to identify food sources. All of these can be refined while on the lake fishing. The analysis gives an indication of the chance of finding fish and offers you a way of seeking fish out on unknown lakes.

5.2 Keep a Technical Log

The log of fishing activity allows you to keep a record of what did (or didn't) work as well as covering when and where questions. It is a simple, effective way of remembering what you normally forget.

So now you know all that we know about trolling for trout. It is hoped that the information helps you understand your quarry a little more and that you have developed a better feel for how to approach that elusive trout. But more than anything, we hope that we have provided you with some information that will help you enjoy the sport. If we have given you even the slightest little bit of additional information that will do this, then we have succeeded in our quest to share the joy of fishing.

Good luck and may your tactics be successful!